KEYS TO RISKS AND REWARDS OF PENNY STOCKS

KEYS TO RISKS AND REWARDS OF PENNY STOCKS

Robert L. Frick

Mary Lynne Vellinga

BARRON'S

All inquiries should be addressed to:
Barron's Educational Series, Inc.
250 Wireless Boulevard
Hauppauge, New York 11788

Library of Congress Catalog Card No. 90-33147

International Standard Book No. 0-8120-4300-6

Library of Congress Cataloging in Publication Data

Frick, Robert L.
    Keys to risks and rewards of penny stocks/Robert L. Frick,
Mary Lynne Vellinga.
      p.   cm.
    ISBN 0-8120-4300-6
    1. Penny stocks. 2. Speculation. I. Vellinga, Mary Lynne.
II. Title.
HG6041.F824 1990
332.63'22--dc20   90-33147
                                            CIP

PRINTED IN THE UNITED STATES OF AMERICA

9012   9770   98765432

CONTENTS

1

INTRODUCTION

Every big corporation in America started as a small company.

The allure of penny stocks is buying a piece of these small companies with hopes of riding them to riches if they grow into large, profitable corporations. Such growth happens often. But finding the right companies to invest in among the thousands on the stock market is not an easy task.

For the most part, the penny stock market is not what it's supposed to be: a conduit through which money from small investors travels to legitimate young companies in need of venture financing. One of the problems is that the same type of people who sold swampland in Florida as prime real estate have attached themselves to the penny stock market, using lies and price manipulation to bilk people out of hundreds of millions of dollars.

In recent years regulators have cracked down on fraudulent penny stock firms, and there is hope that the tide is turning toward a safer and healthier market for low-priced stocks. But even without regulatory protection you can learn to avoid investing in fraudulent and/or worthless companies and, through analysis, research, and common sense, find good small companies to invest in.

Although the authors of this book believe exciting, profitable opportunities are always available in penny stocks, they also believe in the Penny Stock Paradox: *Penny stocks are sold to those least prepared to own them.* We say "sold to" instead of "bought by" because a penny stock transaction most often involves a stockbroker selling to a client, instead of an investor actively researching and shopping for a penny stock purchase. By "least prepared" we mean least prepared financially and educationally. Small investors often are convinced that penny stocks are a surefire ticket to wealth, and thus spend an unreasonably high proportion of their savings on them. Also, understanding penny stocks and especially the market in which penny stocks are traded involves some specialized knowledge that makes penny stock investing in some ways more complex than buying stock in established public companies.

In light of the Penny Stock Paradox, this book outlines not only methods of analyzing penny stocks but also how investors can protect themselves from penny stock fraud, from overinvesting in penny stocks, and from a host of other pitfalls waiting for them. Put even more simply, this book offers ways to reduce risk in penny stock investing. In fact, two sections are devoted to risk, a key at the beginning that discusses different types of risk and ways of reducing risk, and a checklist at the end that summarizes risk factors.

This book is organized in 50 short keys, each explaining a specific topic or giving an example. As such, these keys can be read randomly or in order. Their order is meant to give readers first a broad knowledge of what a penny stock is, what abuses to look out for, and what other factors deserve careful consideration before actually investing any money. Two key issues are risk and diversification. Next is a section on reading financial statements to find out how sound a company is. These lessons are wrapped together in several examples. Finally, some miscellaneous but important topics are covered, including how to extricate yourself from a bad penny stock investment. After the keys there is a question and answer section and a glossary.

We hope this book will help investors take control of their penny stock portfolios, so as not to be led by those in the market who would bilk them. Best of luck.

2

WHAT ARE PENNY STOCKS?

A penny stock is usually defined as the stock of a young, public company, often with an erratic or nonexistent sales and earnings history, that trades at a very low price and is not listed on any stock exchange. "Cheap" is defined variously as under $1 a share to under $5 per share. But as we will see in Key 35, price is irrelevant. The most important part of the definition of penny stocks is that these companies have yet to put together a stable, dependable business.

This is a broad definition and includes many different types of companies in many stages of development. To broaden the definition further, the authors include stocks of small companies that aren't young but are in a state of flux. Some companies, described as "turnaround" situations, have made money in the past but now find themselves in trouble. Maybe they went too far into debt, or a competitor came out with a superior product.

Without stability and dependability there is risk.

But with risk there is also the potential for great reward.

Some penny stock companies can be doing well, but because they are small or in a mundane business, they are lost among the thousands of other stocks on the market. Often the prices of these "wallflower" stocks do not reflect what the business is really worth. On the one hand, this could be an investment opportunity; on the other hand, if you invest in such a company, you run the risk that the stock price will never reflect what you think the company's value is.

3

NASDAQ AND THE PINK SHEETS

Penny stocks are generally considered to be stocks traded "over the counter"—that is, they are not listed or traded on an organized exchange such as the New York Stock Exchange or the American Stock Exchange. Many OTC stocks can be found on the National Association of Securities Dealers Automated Quotation System, or NASDAQ. This system provides current stock price information to over 3,000 computers in the offices of securities firms and financial institutions nationwide. Through their computer terminals, market makers enter the highest price at which they are willing to buy a security or the lowest price at which they are willing to sell it. As of 1989 over 4,000 companies had stock listed on NASDAQ.

Regulators generally don't include NASDAQ-traded stocks in their definition of "penny stocks." But the most financially solid low-priced stocks are likely to be NASDAQ listed, so they are in our definition.

Many thousand more companies aren't members of the NASDAQ system, either because they don't meet NASDAQ's financial requirements or because they choose not to pursue a listing, which carries with it certain reporting requirements. Low-priced stocks not listed on NASDAQ or any exchange are commonly known as "pink sheet" stocks. The prices of these stocks are not quoted electronically. Instead, they are negotiated over the phone among brokers. One private company, the National Quotation Bureau Inc. of Jersey City, N.J., prints a daily list of brokerage firms trading in about 16,000 over-the-counter stocks and the price quotes they give. About 11,000 of the stocks are non-NASDAQ. The circular is pink, hence the name "pink sheets."

Price information about pink sheet stocks is not easy to come by. For one thing, the pink sheets are not distributed to the general public. Most brokers subscribe to them, and some newspapers also publish penny stock prices. Another problem is that the prices listed in the pink sheets aren't necessarily the actual market prices. In fact, the pink sheet listings are paid advertisements placed by brokerage firms who want other brokers to see that they are willing to buy or sell a particular security. Thus, not all the brokerage firms trading a stock will necessarily be listed.

Companies traded on NASDAQ offer investors some advantages over pink sheet stocks:

- Price information is quoted on electronic screens across the country and thus is more easily accessible to investors.
- NASDAQ has some minimum requirements for its companies. In order to obtain a NASDAQ listing a company must have at least $2 million in assets and $1 million in shareholders' equity. (Assets may fall as low as $750,000 and equity as low as $375,000 before a company is delisted, however.) In contrast, the National Quotation Bureau re-

quires only that the brokerage firms listed in its publication and the securities they trade be registered with the U.S. Securities and Exchange Commission or be exempt from registration requirements. (Exempt companies include foreign firms and small companies incorporated prior to 1933.)

- NASDAQ requires a company to have at least two market makers before its stock can be listed. Once a stock is listed, however, it needs only one market maker to retain that listing. An average NASDAQ stock has 10.7 market makers. Only one market maker is needed to list a stock on the pink sheets.
- Market makers in NASDAQ stocks must report trading volume at the end of each day. For heavier volume stocks listed in the National Market System portion of NASDAQ, volume must be reported 90 seconds after a trade is completed. In contrast, firms trading pink sheet stocks have to report volume to the NASD only if they trade more than $10,000 worth, or more than 50,000 shares, of a company's stock in one day.

Because of this lack of reporting rules, stock price manipulation is more easily achieved in the pink sheet market. Indeed, many brokerage houses disassociate themselves from their pink sheet brethren by saying that they trade only those low-priced stocks listed on NASDAQ. But a NASDAQ listing is certainly no guarantee of legitimacy. Because a stock need have only one market maker to remain on the system, the potential for manipulation of small stocks by one or two brokerage houses is still very much present.

4

HISTORY OF PENNY STOCKS

It is widely believed that penny stocks originated as shares sold in western gold and silver mines during the 1800s. Because mining required such a large capital investment, few prospectors could go it alone. So they turned to the public for funds. Promoters of oil and gas concerns followed; and, since that time, different types of firms have been in vogue, most recently high-tech stocks and blind pools or blank check companies (Key 41).

Given the history of penny stocks, it's not surprising that the western cities of Denver and Salt Lake City have long been centers of activity for this market. Indeed, some have even been presumptuous enough to call Denver "Wall Street West."

While these two cities are still penny stock hubs, modern telecommunications has enabled the business to spread across the country. In 1989 there were 325 penny stock brokerage houses in 29 states, up from 55 in six states five years ago, according to a report by the North American Securities Administrators Association (NASAA). Some 20,000 to 30,000 stocks trade over the counter but are not listed on the National Association of Securities Dealers Automated Quotation System. Most of these are found only in the "pink sheets," the daily listing of companies and their market makers.

Not all the stocks found in the pink sheets are penny stocks, but virtually all penny stocks are found in the pink sheets. Many are priced at less than $1 a share, but the business adds up to much more than pennies. Regulators estimate that $10 billion worth of penny stocks are traded each year. In addition, many of the 4,300 stocks that trade over the counter on NASDAQ are priced at less than $5 a share.

Unfortunately, the enormous growth in the penny stock market has been accompanied by a boom in penny stock fraud. Many companies that sell stock to the public have no operating business and no intention of trying to build one. NASAA estimates that penny stock frauds bilk Americans out of $2 billion a year. Regulators are presently engaged in a crackdown aimed at cleaning up the industry.

That con artists should choose penny stocks as a vehicle is not surprising, given the market's roots in mining and oil and gas stocks. Regulators say the first penny stock fraud dates back at least to the 1940s and 50s, when worthless shares in uranium mine stocks were bought and sold over the counter of a Salt Lake City coffee shop. But it is only within the past decade that penny stock fraud has grown beyond its regional constraints to become a truly national problem.

Today's penny stock scams have included, but have by no means been confined to, mining outfits. They run the gamut from AIDS cures to razor blades. Regulators are especially concerned about blank check/blind pool companies, which are corporate shells that have no operating business and often are created solely for fraudulent purposes.

5

RISK

Investing in penny stocks means you have made a decision to take a high risk with your money. The odds of losing are high. If a broker or anyone else tells you otherwise, don't believe it. The North American Securities Administrators Association has estimated that in a penny stock market *without* manipulation, investors will lose all or some of their money 70% of the time. NASAA also estimates that with the market manipulation of recent years, that loss figure has jumped to 90%. Poor odds indeed! Investors would be better off going to Las Vegas and betting all their penny stock investment money at the roulette wheel on "red." At least then the odds of winning would be about 50%.

Of course, the NASAA figures are for *all* penny stocks, and the purpose of this book is to help readers steer clear of not only the penny stocks being manipulated, but also the legitimate investments that are highly unlikely to succeed. Savvy investors can turn the odds much more heavily in their favor.

Even with good screening, penny stocks are still a risky investment. But for taking a higher risk you're

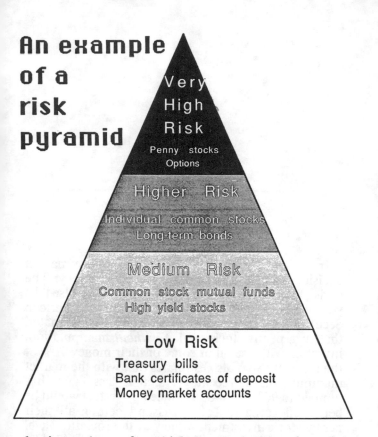

An example of a risk pyramid

Very High Risk
Penny stocks
Options

Higher Risk
Individual common stocks
Long-term bonds

Medium Risk
Common stock mutual funds
High yield stocks

Low Risk
Treasury bills
Bank certificates of deposit
Money market accounts

buying a chance for a higher reward. When financial advisors try to find out how much risk a client is willing to take, they sometimes show a chart similar to the one on this page. At the bottom of the "risk pyramid" are very safe investments, which will yield a low but dependable rate of return. The higher on the risk pyramid, the higher the rate of return, but the more chance you will get no return at all or will lose all your money. Notice that penny stocks are at the pinnacle of the risk pyramid.

Before deciding how much of your money you want to invest in penny stocks, you need to ask yourself how much risk are you willing to bear. Look at all of your investments—your entire portfolio—and decide what portion you want to expose in a high risk area. Generally, investment advisors suggest no more than 5% to 10% of an average investor's portfolio be in high risk investments, so if all that money is lost, the blow will not be too severe.

The amount of risk one investor finds tolerable may be intolerable for another. Thus, you should mix and match investments in different proportions to find a risk level you are comfortable with. For instance, Joe Investor might satisfy his risk level by placing $2,000 of his $20,000 portfolio (10%) in penny stocks and the rest in bank certificates of deposit. Or, he might invest $5,000 in a stock mutual fund—more money but in a much less risky investment—and the remainder in bank products.

One caution: If Joe Investor's penny stocks suddenly tripled in value, he would be tempted to place even more money in penny stocks. But just because he scored once, doesn't mean penny stock investing has become any less risky. He would do better to cash in part of his penny stocks, thus keeping them at 10% of his portfolio.

Here is a list of risks you should consider when investing. When you learn to recognize these 4 risks, you can work to minimize them:

1. *Psychological risk:* It is important to know the level of risk you personally can tolerate with your investments. By matching your investments to your psychological risk level, you can enjoy or feel secure with your investing, instead of dreading it or being frustrated by it.

2. *Market risk:* When the stock market rises and falls because of broad, unpredictable, or uncontrollable factors—such as war, interest rate swings, federal budget problems—it is called market risk. This is the risk that all investors in the stock market must learn to live with. The October 1987 Black Monday market crash is a good example.
3. *Firm-unique risk:* Putting all your hopes into one stock is a mistake. There are many factors that affect a firm's fortunes, such as demand for its product, competence of managers, and competition, and it's easy for something to go wrong even in the best of companies. Diversification, covered in Key 6, can help minimize firm-unique risk.
4. *Broker risk:* A brokerage firm could be manipulating a stock's price for its own profit, or making unauthorized transactions with your account. While this risk can be present any time you invest in stocks, it is more prevalent in the penny stock market. Methods to reduce broker risk are discussed in Key 9.

6

DIVERSIFICATION

Diversification simply means spreading your money among different investments. It is a classic method for reducing risk. The more stocks you invest in, the smaller the risk, generally speaking, but the smaller your chance for high returns. For instance, investors wanting to match the performance of the entire stock market can buy stock mutual funds that own hundreds of stocks. But because the stock market generally doesn't rise and fall as quickly as individual stocks, the chance for greater gains (or losses) is reduced.

When buying stocks, you can diversify by purchasing stocks in different industries. A portfolio with nothing but stocks in auto companies will swing with the fortunes of that industry. But a portfolio with auto, bank, food, and energy stocks will be more stable because while the fortunes of some industries may be falling, the prospects of another may be rising. True diversification involves not only buying different stocks, but also putting money into several different *types* of investments: stocks, bonds, real estate, and money market accounts, etc.

Because most penny stock investors seek risk, too much diversification among penny stocks defeats the goal of assuming a high risk for a chance at a high reward. For instance, if you invest an equal amount in ten penny stocks, and one stock increases in price tenfold but the others go bust, your portfolio will just break even.

There are practical considerations, too. If you decide you only want to commit $2,000 or $3,000 to penny stocks, you cannot buy many stocks and therefore cannot get well diversified. And unless you can devote a great deal of time to your penny stock investments, you may consider buying stock in only one or two companies and following them closely. As will become increasingly apparent as you read this book, following the fortunes of penny stock companies is more difficult and, therefore, more time-consuming than following bigger, established companies.

Finally, because the price of a penny stock company is often supported by only one or two brokerage firms, if one of these firms went out of business, it could be disastrous for some stock prices—at least in the short term. Thus, buying stocks that have the support of different firms can reduce your dependence on the health of a single brokerage firm.

7

THE COLD CALL

Here is how most investors are introduced to penny stocks: One evening the phone rings in your home. You pick it up, and on the other end of the line is someone who calls himself or herself a stockbroker. Many brokerage firms, not only those selling penny stocks, rely heavily on such "cold calls" to solicit new customers.

Of course, while they can be annoying, many of these calls are made by legitimate firms trying to drum up business. But the telephone is also a handy tool for boiler room operators who use high-pressure sales tactics to lure investors into worthless stocks. Modern phone systems have helped fraud flourish like never before.

One example of an aggressive cold-call system was that used by the now defunct F. D. Roberts Securities Inc. According to a report by the North American Securities Administrators Association, brokers at the firm were told that if they stayed on the phone badgering prospects for 12 to 18 hours a day, they would end up "dirty, filthy, stinking rich." Here's how the typical cold-call strategy works:

- On the first call, the broker takes a low-key approach. He tells you he has been making an awful lot of money for his clients, and asks if you would like him to call you when he has a stock with good potential. Well, you don't have anything to lose, you think, so you say yes.
- On the second call, the broker says he thinks he has a situation that might be right for you. Could you just tell him how much you make and how much you have available to invest?
- The third call is the hook. The broker tells you he has stock available in XYZ Co., a firm that's just going public. He describes it as having great prospects. He may claim inside knowledge of the company, saying it is about to announce a huge new contract or merge with another firm. He may also promise a specific return—say 50%—on your investment. When you ask for some written information about the company and its financial condition, like a prospectus, he promises to send you what he has—but says you don't have time to wait for it. You have to invest now, or miss out, because he has only a limited number of shares left.

This last call is a red flag. Your broker has just violated securities law. It is illegal for anyone to promise you specific returns on stock or to trade on insider information about a company. Brokerage firms also are required to have prospectuses available when soliciting investors in new issues.

The high-pressure phone sales operator will probably act warm and friendly, addressing you frequently by name to make you feel that there is a personal bond between the two of you. But don't expect any favors. In actuality, your name may just be one in hundreds that this broker has plugged into a script he holds in his hand.

Following is an example of such a script. It was presented as evidence in a civil class action suit against Power Securities Corp., a Las Vegas-based penny stock firm that went out of business in February 1989, leaving thousands of investors around the country holding virtually worthless securities. Power was the subject of regulatory actions in a number of states before it closed. According to lawyers representing investors in the case, this script was obtained from a former Power broker. It concerns a merger between Davin Enterprises Inc., a public blind pool (see page 28), and Target Vision Inc., a company selling video information services.

"Mr. *Prospect,* I'm working with a major recommendation. The name of the company is Davin Enterprises. Davin just merged with a Rochester company called Target Vision. Unbelievable local interest. Target Vision is a state-of-the-art information and communication company. They provide information and delivery systems using closed circuit television. Right now, Mr. *Prospect,* these systems are being used in hotels, colleges, hospitals, car dealerships and factories. Growing rapidly. You have 24 hour 365 day news, weather, sports and financial updates.

"Mr. *Prospect,* Merrill Lynch invested 1.5 million dollars into Target Vision (and) they're looking for 10 to 15 times their investment. The way I see it, if it's good enough for Merrill Lynch it's definitely good enough for me and my clients. You get my point, don't you? (wait for response) Great!!!! Let's pick up——— shares at ten cents a share . . ."

Investors who listened to this sales pitch would have been sadly misled. The merger between Davin and Target Vision had not gone through, and, indeed, never did go through. Nor did the broker mention that Target Vision was losing large sums of money, straining the budget of its then parent company, Sportecular Inc. In fiscal 1987, before the planned merger with Davin was announced, Target Vision lost $2.1 million on revenues of $423,166. As of spring

1989, with Power closed, Davin stock was virtually worthless.

Regulators have been searching for ways to protect investors from such losses. New rules approved by the SEC in the summer of 1989 are designed to soften high-pressure boiler room tactics used to persuade inexperienced investors to buy penny stocks over the phone. The rules, which took effect in January 1990, involve only small penny stocks priced at under $5 a share and not listed on the National Association of Securities Dealers Automated Quotation System. Under the rules, a new customer must give written approval for the purchase of such penny stocks. The broker also must make a written determination of why the investment is suitable for the customer, and obtain a document signed by the customer outlining his or her financial situation and investment goals.

How effective the new rules will be remains to be seen. In the meantime, regulators say the best way to protect yourself is by remembering this old saying: If somebody offers you something that sounds too good to be true, it probably is. The National Association of Securities Dealers advises people never to buy investments over the phone without having met their broker first.

8

MANIPULATION

Naturally, no penny stock underwriter wants to see the stock it has brought public drop below the offering price. An underwriter is judged by the success of its deals. And if the bottom falls out of the market after the offering, the brokerage will have a hard time finding customers to sell the stock to, thus drying up a source of commissions.

However, sometimes a brokerage firm's efforts to support a stock become tantamount to "market manipulation," a situation not uncommon in the penny stock market. David S. Ruder, former chairman of the SEC, has defined market manipulation as an artificial scheme designed to affect the price (almost always to raise it) and the trading volume of the target securities. Penny stocks are especially susceptible to manipulation because they are often thinly traded and dominated by one or two market making brokerage firms.

To perpetuate a manipulation scheme, a brokerage firm needs ranks of brokers to call potential customers en masse and pitch the stock to them. The sales pitches are often misleading or even false. One frequent ploy is to buy back thousands of shares of stock from one group of customers at one price while simultaneously selling to another group of investors at a higher price. Cases have shown that penny stock operators will even resort to writing false press releases or financial statements to pump up the price of a stock.

While the specifics of manipulation schemes vary, the SEC has defined these frequently recurring elements:

Phase one of the manipulation begins with a "shell company," which can either be a public company whose operating business has become defunct or a "blind pool" or "blank check" company, which has raised money from investors by saying it plans to acquire some unidentified business.

In phase two, the promoters place the stock in what are known as "friendly hands," which can be actual friends or family. Sometimes the stock is given to these "investors" at no charge. The idea here is to have enough shareholders so that a legitimate market can be said to exist. Meanwhile, the promoters will themselves own, or secretly control through these "friendly" customers, large quantities of stock. Thus they stand to make hefty profits if the stock price rises.

Now comes the merger. The shell company is frequently merged with a private company described as having great potential. Some recently fashionable businesses have involved AIDS cures, uranium, or that long-time favorite, gold. These shell offerings (see Key 41) are often organized and orchestrated by promoters who are habitual securities law violators. They are in turn aided by a cadre of attorneys, accountants, public relations firms, and transfer agents who provide legal opinions, certify financial statements, provide publicity, and transfer stock certificates.

Enter the broker. In order to boost the price of a

company's shares in the secondary market, the promoters need a brokerage firm with hundreds of brokers to extol the company's virtues to potential investors. Promoters may give the brokerage firm stock or cash in exchange for its services as a market maker in the stock. The broker-dealer firm may have an ongoing relationship with the promoter.

To create the appearance of a legitimate market, the primary market maker may arrange for other firms to list themselves as market makers. In return, the first firm may agree to return the favor in the future or to pay the second market maker a fee for its services.

Now the stage is set. The brokerage firm purchases the stock in large blocks for sale to the public at predetermined prices. Then the brokers get on the phones, making high-pressure sales pitches to thousands of investors each day. The brokers are often naïve young people who simply read the misleading scripts provided to them by their brokerage firm, sometimes unaware that they are perpetuating a fraud on investors.

Because one brokerage firm dominates trading in the stock, it can charge investors excessive markups. Meanwhile, the original promoters profit by selling their stock at hugely inflated prices.

After the stock reaches a certain price—say, four cents—the brokerage firm may buy it back from customers and flip it to another broker-dealer for further manipulation. This last group of customers is unlikely to receive cash for its shares, however. The brokers will most likely try and convince their customers to trade the shares for stock in another worthless company. Eventually, new buyers for the worthless stock can no longer be found and the scheme collapses.

In a manipulated market, the investor stands very little chance of profiting. The price of the stock may seem high, but it is really an artificial price set by the brokerage firm. You may find the market suddenly takes a tumble if you want to sell your shares and receive cash. Your broker may even tell you the market can't absorb the sale of your shares. He may stop taking your phone calls.

Using the muscle of hundreds of salespeople, penny stock brokerage firms can create ridiculously high market values for companies with no profits and virtually no operations at all. In one case a mining company whose entire assets consisted of one pick-up truck was touted as having had 1987 gold sales of more than $4.5 million.

Overpriced shares usually tumble if the brokerage firm promoting them gets in trouble with regulators. Scores of penny stock firms are shut down by regulators each year, and the big losers are usually investors.

After Power Securities Corp. closed in February 1989 under pressure from regulators, one investor (who had never invested in the stock market before) lamented to a reporter that he had lost his entire life savings with Power, most of it in a stock called Star Publications Inc. His $49,417 investment in Star Publications stock had become worthless. (The case of Star Publications is described in more detail in Key 39.)

Unfortunately, this investor and many others learned too late that a little investigation would have saved a lot of grief.

9

BROKERS: GOOD AND BAD

The kind of broker and brokerage firm you choose can make or break you in the penny stock market. Be sure you check out both carefully. One problem is that many penny stock firms hire brokers with little or no experience. Some firms even recruit young people by the hundreds and put them through a crash course so they can pass the test qualifying them to sell stock. These recruits are prized for their salesmanship, not for their stock market savvy. Retail salespeople, grocery checkout clerks, bar bouncers—all of these people can become brokers within a matter of weeks. You may want someone with more experience handling your account.

Ask your broker how long he or she has been in the brokerage business, for whom he has worked, how many customers she has. If your account is small, you may want to settle for someone who has less experience and fewer customers but will give your investments more attention.

Here are five questions to ask yourself when choosing a broker and when evaluating the performance of your present broker.

1. Does your broker seem knowledgeable about the stock he's selling, or does he merely appear to be reading from a "script?"
2. Is she pushing you to invest all your extra cash in penny stocks, or cautioning that you should have more conservative investments as well?
3. Is she pressuring you to buy right away, or providing you with enough written information so you can make intelligent investment decisions?
4. Is it easy to sell your stock when you want to, or does your broker pressure you to hold on?
5. Have you been able to get cash profits out of your investments?

You can find out a broker's employment and disciplinary history by contacting the National Association of Securities Dealers. (The same method can be used to discover the disciplinary history of a firm.) Investors are allowed two free information requests every three months. In order to make such an inquiry, you must first obtain an information request form by calling the NASD at (301) 590-6500 or by writing P.O. Box 9401, Gaithersburg, Maryland 20898-9401. Address letters to the attention of the public disclosure program. You also should check with your state securities division to make sure the broker you're dealing with is registered to sell securities in your state.

Most regulators advise that you meet a broker before investing. Be on your guard during that meeting, and don't worry about making your broker like you. Dishonest brokers sometimes appear far more trusting and honest than honest brokers. And the better you get to know them, the more easily they may convince you to open your wallet. Investors are often impressed by brokers who wear lavish clothes and drive fancy cars. But remember, their customers are paying for those luxuries.

It's also important to check out the brokerage firm you're dealing with. A well-intentioned but naîve broker working for a dishonest firm can inadvertently dupe you. Managers have been known to give their brokers misleading or false information about the stocks they are selling. Young brokers without much experience may not realize that their firm is manipulating a stock or engaging in other fraudulent activity. They may be as surprised as their customers when their firm is disciplined by regulators or, in some cases, goes out of business.

Talk to family, friends, and colleagues to see what brokerage firm they recommend and whether they've had trouble with a particular one. Call around to different brokerage firms to find one whose style seems right for you. Because of the high failure rate of penny stock firms, you probably should be cautious about investing with a firm that has only been in existence for a year or two.

10

FIRST STEPS

Now that you have a basic knowledge of penny stocks and the penny stock markets, the next question becomes one of which stocks to buy.

One route, of course, is to find a broker you trust to make good recommendations, and then screen those recommendations. But if you have the time and the interest, it makes sense to do your own initial research —even though getting started can seem a daunting task.

Many investment experts say the first rule is to stick to what you know, understand, and like. Don't underestimate yourself. Look to your profession and hobbies for some expertise already in your head, then apply that expertise to picking stocks. For example, if you work in a restaurant, there are plenty of public restaurant and food product companies to choose from. If the company you work for has a supplier you think does an outstanding job, find out if the supplier is a public company. Another good starting point is companies in your own community. You can easily keep tabs on their performance in local newspapers and through direct contacts.

Once you've established an interest in certain industries or individual companies, you can look for relevant information in the articles and stock tables printed in penny stock newspapers. (As a rule the general financial media don't give much coverage to penny stocks.) You'll notice in penny stock newspapers advertisements placed by firms that promise, for a fee, expert recommendations on penny stock prospects. You should be leery of such offers. Regulators occasionally discover that these firms take either advertising or direct payments from the firms they recommend. If that's not disclosed, it's illegal. Even if it is disclosed, you must wonder how objective the recommendations can be. In addition, some of these newsletter "experts" may have investments in the companies they are recommending.

On the other hand, newsletters that supply condensed financial information and business descriptions on a number of companies can save you a great deal of time in your search for interesting companies. So, listen to their advice, but check out each recommendation carefully. Build up folders of information on each firm until you have enough information to intelligently choose from among them. The larger your universe of choices, the better those choices will be.

Be sure to track not just a company's performance, but its stock price, too. You may discover that the stock trades within a certain range—say between $1.00 and $1.50 per share. If you do decide to buy, you can instruct your broker to buy at no more than $1.00 a share.

Once you have a few good candidates, check out the brokerage firms who deal in the stock. If you have the patience, before making purchases choose some stocks to put an imaginary portfolio. "Trade" these and other stocks for a few months to get a taste of what real investing is like before taking the plunge.

But above all, take control of your own investing.

11

SPREADS AND MARKUPS

In the stock market the "spread" is the difference between what a brokerage firm will pay for a stock (the bid price) and what it will sell it for (the ask price). The spreads on low-priced stocks can be wide—300% or more—and you should be aware of them.

While spreads and markups aren't the same thing, a very wide spread may indicate that your broker is charging you a fat markup (or markdown, if you're selling) as well.

When a firm "makes a market" in a stock and sells shares to you directly out of its inventory, it is acting in a "principal" capacity. In this case, the commission you pay will not be listed separately on your order confirmation. The stock price was "marked up" by a certain percentage to pay the broker and the brokerage house.

On a given day your broker may be selling stock in the XYZ Co. at ten cents a share but be paying only five cents for it. This means that if you bought the stock at ten cents that day, you might be able to get only five cents for it moments later. While a five-cent difference may not seem like much, it translates into a spread of 100%. That means your stock would have to double in price just for you to break even.

One thing to keep in mind when deciding whether a spread is too high: Penny stocks can double in price much more quickly than their higher-priced counterparts. Spreads are largely determined by supply and demand. Like any merchant, the brokerage doesn't have to take a large markup to make money on a high-volume item. But it may take a higher markup to cover the carrying costs of a stock that languishes on its "shelves."

The market for a heavily traded stock with many market makers usually is more competitive. For example, one market maker might be offering to sell the stock at $2.00, and buy it at $1.00, but another broker wanting a piece of the action could come in and offer to buy shares at $1.25 and sell them for $1.75, thus luring customers away from the first firm.

A company's stock may be thinly traded—and thus have wider spreads—for a variety of reasons: The majority of the stock could be held by company insiders, who tend not to trade many shares. Or the stock could be infrequently traded because its holders view it as a long-term investment. Or it could be that the company arouses little interest among investors because it is doing poorly. Even popular stocks sometimes carry wide spreads, a situation that often means that most of the shares are controlled by one or two market makers.

To obtain a listing on the NASDAQ electronic quotation system, a company must have at least two market makers in its stock. But it can maintain their NASDAQ listing even if only one market maker keeps trading the stock. A wide spread can be a telltale sign of stock manipulation.

Even these minimal requirements don't exist for unlisted stocks quoted in the "pink sheets," published by the private National Quotation Bureau Inc. Pink sheet stocks tend to have higher spreads than those listed on NASDAQ. In the electronic system, the best bids and offers for a stock are displayed on thousands of computer terminals in brokerage houses around the country, making prices and spreads relatively easy to track. But in the pink sheet market, where quotes are given over the phone by individual market makers, the spreads are harder to track and may vary widely from firm to firm.

If your firm is not a market maker in the stock, your broker will have to call up firms that are and buy the stock from one of them. Here, your firm is acting in an "agency" capacity and will charge you a set fee, or commission, for the transaction.

In general, NASD guidelines prohibit broker-dealers from marking a stock up more than 5% over the prevailing market price. The SEC also prohibits brokerage firms from charging excessive, undisclosed markups.

12

SOURCES OF INFORMATION

A reference tool to help you research low-priced companies is probably only as far away as the public library. Here's a list of guides to over-the-counter stock.

The *National Stock Summary,* known as the Blue Book, is published semiannually by the National Quotation Bureau Inc., the same company that compiles the pink sheets. Probably the most inclusive source you'll find, the blue book contains information on about 20,000 companies, the same ones listed in the pink sheets. This includes companies traded over-the-counter both on and off the NASDAQ system. Information includes:

The company's name and address
The number of shares it has outstanding
Any dividends
Information on outstanding warrants
Details of the initial public offering and any subsequent offerings
Recent price ranges
Stock splits

In addition, the authors will include information on a bankruptcy filing when they are informed of it. You can obtain historical price information about small stocks by writing to the National Quotation Bureau Inc., Plaza Three, Harborside Financial Center, Jersey City, NJ 07302. (You will be charged a fee, however.)

Standard & Poor's publishes a number of reference works containing information on over-the-counter stocks. These listings generally are limited to actively traded stocks, thus excluding many smaller companies. They include:

- Standard & Poor's *Daily Stock Price Record,* published four times a year, provides a daily and weekly price record for 5,700 over-the-counter stocks.
- *OTC Stock Reports* contains information on 1,500 actively traded stocks in the OTC market and regional stock exchanges. The reports include recent price range, price-to-earnings ratio, dividends paid, yield, S&P ranking of the firm, and summaries of the company's business, earnings, and important historical developments.
- *OTC ProFiles,* published three times a year, contains similar information on more than 750 stocks traded on NASDAQ and U.S. and Canadian regional exchanges. These firms are generally smaller and less actively traded than those covered in the larger *OTC Stock Reports.*

The Market Guide: Over the Counter Stock Edition, published by Market Guide Inc. in Glen Head, N.Y., contains research reports on 800 over-the-counter companies the authors think could be good buys. They are chosen for one or more of the following sets of characteristics:

- Average monthly volume of more than 100,000 shares, a bid price of more than $1, a price-to-

earnings ratio of less than 25, and positive revenue and earnings growth.
- No long-term debt, a current ratio of greater than 3.5, and positive earnings before interest and taxes.
- Yields of 10% or more.
- A three-year track record of more than 150% annual growth in sales along with positive earnings growth.

This guide includes many stocks priced under $5 and even under $3. Some of the reports seem somewhat out of date, however. And while they can aid you in your search for promising stocks, books such as this can't substitute for your own research on the current state of a company and its historical performance.

Newspapers, magazines, and newsletters that specialize in penny stocks can also provide leads. But you should check out any information you get from such sources because some of them don't spend much time investigating promoters' claims. Be especially skeptical of articles sent to you by your broker, who obviously has a vested interest in convincing you to buy the stock.

Investors in Star Publications learned this lesson the hard way. A March 1988 article in *Speculators* magazine claimed the company had the marketing rights to a new type of disposable, collapsible razor and even gave a phone number that prospective investors could call to receive a free razor. But at that time a California firm, International Telesynergistics, was insisting that it actually held those rights. Its claim was upheld in a September 1988 arbitration proceeding, and investors holding Star Publications stock were dismayed to find that their company's major product had vanished. These investors could have checked out the magazine's claims by obtaining financial documents Star had filed with the SEC that detailed the legal dispute over the marketing rights.

13

WHEN TO BUY

Dozens of different strategies exist for when to buy stocks—during market lulls, when hemlines rise, if a stock is making successive new highs, and so on.

The key to deciding when to buy penny stocks is to ignore such distractions and to buy based on fundamental analysis of a company's financial statements, products, and management.

In contrast, some strategists base their trading on price behavior of individual stocks and the stock market in general. Many investors take cues from the general market to make purchases. If the market is in a rally, they may buy, for instance. Later, they may try to sell when they feel the market is peaking.

The market for penny stocks differs greatly from the market for the stocks of major companies followed in widely quoted market measures such as the Dow Jones Industrial Average and the Standard & Poor's Composite Index of 500 Stocks. These measures are made up of selected stocks from the New York Stock Exchange, the American Stock Exchange, and, selectively, NASDAQ.

Trading in these stocks is dominated by large institutional investors such as mutual fund companies, pension funds, and insurance companies. These institutions don't deal in penny stocks for a variety of reasons, risk and the pennies' small size being two of the biggest. Thus, when the "Dow" or the "S&P 500" jump, tumble, or crawl, penny stocks seem largely oblivious. Low-price-stock traders say it takes events as cataclysmic as the October 1987 stock market crash to affect trading in penny stocks.

Because of the higher risk and often the lack of a healthy market, each penny stock operates in a world all its own. This is both a strength and weakness for penny stocks. If a cheaply priced venture company blossoms into a thriving entity, its stock will be noticed by many investors and the price will skyrocket no matter what the larger market is doing. On the other hand, a penny stock company with moderate but unspectacular progress might not attract attention and thus will not increase in price.

As an investor, you might be tempted to buy a stock in a biotech company because biotechnology is making headlines. Resist the temptation. Penny stock underwriters have been known to bring issues to market that have little fundamental value except for matching what's hot in the headlines. Such sectors as oil and gas, genetic engineering, and gold mining have been popular topics for such exploitation.

Another dangerous time to buy is right after a penny stock company goes public. Often these stocks initially trade to huge premiums and then fall back. This will be discussed further in Key 42.

If you're wavering on a stock, the time to buy might be when company insiders buy stock, or when someone acquires more than 5% of the company, meaning a takeover may be imminent.

The last word belongs to a long-time penny stock broker: "If you buy quality, you never get hurt."

14

WHEN TO SELL

Many investment experts say knowing when to sell stock is much harder than knowing when to buy it. People sell stock for many reasons: to take profits, to limit losses, to switch to a better investment, or to bail out because they need the money. Investment experts have different strategies for selling, but operating emotionally isn't one of them. Don't become emotionally attached to a stock.

Here are some strategies and tips on when to sell:

- Sell if you wouldn't buy the stock at the current price. Presumably you made the decision to buy partly based on price (Key 35); use the same analysis to determine when the stock is overpriced.
- Especially if you are a short-term trader, sell enough stock to make back the money you initially invested, with a significant number of shares left over. This strategy can build a portfolio of "free stock," and could work well with a string of initial public offerings—which usually trade to a quick premium.
- Sell when company insiders sell big blocks of their own stock, and have no good reason for the sale. If

an insider tells you the stock was sold to reinvest in the company, check it out. Such a reinvestment must show up as "paid-in capital" or a loan on a balance sheet.

- Sell when a better low-price stock comes along, and you don't want to increase the proportion of penny stocks in your investment portfolio.

Consider selling when:

- The price drops. Be aware that this may also be a signal to buy more stock at a bargain, so check out the reason for the drop. But set a price at which you wouldn't want to absorb more losses, and stick to it. Let your broker know this price, and give instructions to sell.
- The spread opens significantly. This is a sign investors have lost interest in the stock, for whatever reason. If the market has abandoned the stock, no matter how much you like it, no one will pay a premium for your shares.
- The number of shares traded drops. Again, a sign other investors have lost interest.
- The company is running out of money and has yet to establish its business. Keep close tabs on the income statements and balance sheets, see Keys 26–28 to gauge the rate at which the company is spending and how many assets it has left to pay the bills. The end often comes before the last dime is spent. Yes, the company may be able to raise more money, but that's not a sure thing.

Do not sell your stock simply because your broker says it's time to buy a new stock or that the price has increased and is unlikely to run up anymore. Demand some fundamental reason why it's wise to sell. Remember that brokers make their living buying and selling stock for clients.

15

SECTORS

When considering an investment in penny stocks, it may be useful to pick an industry you think shows promise and to look for stocks within that industry. While sector analysis should not be your only tool for picking stocks—you still need to consider each company on its own merits—it can be helpful in narrowing down the list of investment alternatives.

Over time, the distribution of stocks in different sectors changes. Sometimes, especially in the penny stock market, these changes seem to be mere fads— AIDS stocks one day, lasers the next. But they also reflect changes in underlying economic forces. For example, the initial offering market for low-priced issues was once dominated by energy stocks. But today, with the price of oil relatively low, the number of companies getting into the business has declined and energy stocks have lost much of their significance. (Some experts think that the demand for energy will outrun the supply in the next ten years, making the 1990s a good decade for oil stocks.)

Because stocks that trade only in the "pink sheets" are not widely followed or analyzed, it is difficult to track such stocks by industry. But a look at the distribution of NASDAQ over-the-counter stocks is also instructive, as many low-priced stocks are traded on NASDAQ.

The table below shows the number of companies in select NASDAQ industry groups and the percentage by which each group grew or shrank during 1988. The table lists the eight fastest-growing and the eight-slowest growing of 34 NASDAQ major industry groups.

Major Industry Groups	% change 12/31/87 to 12/30/88	Number of Companies
Telecommunications	+43.8 percent	101
Medical instruments and supplies	+36.7	123
Machinery	+31.2	103
Apparel	+29.1	62
Primary manufacturing	+28.4	158
Wholesale trade	+27.3	152
Food products	+26.1	70
Trucking and transportation	+24.8	107
And here are the laggards:		
Gold and silver	−15.1	39
Oil and gas	−12.3	151
Electronic components	−9.6	111
Pharmaceuticals	−2.7	117
Commercial banks and bank holding companies in the Southwest	+0.3	24
Computer manufacturers	+0.3	194
Electrical equipment	+4.5	83
Business services	+4.8	146

16

HIGH TECHNOLOGY

High tech stocks have replaced mining and energy stocks as the leaders of the penny stock market. The brokerage firms that eagerly latch on to what they see as the latest fad have recognized the appeal of high tech businesses. So it's necessary to exercise extreme caution when investing in this area.

Surely, though, there are legitimate high-tech firms out there in need of capital. This key should help you identify them.

Just what does "high tech" mean? One useful definition of the term is a company on the leading edge of its particular industry, whether it be computers or medicine, optics or farm machinery. These entrepreneurs are expanding the frontiers of our technology and providing a means for economic growth in the future.

Reading a prospectus issued by a high-tech company can be rough going. For instance, the November 1988 prospectus for Antigenics Inc., an AIDS research firm, claimed that the company, in conjunction with the University of Toronto, had developed "a series of synthetic immunoadsorbents for use in a therapeutic apheresis device designed to absorb specific immune complexes from circulating blood." At this point many investors would have given up. Others would have become more interested, however, impressed by jargon that sounds complex and technical.

It's impossible to evaluate a company's potential unless you can grasp the meaning of its business. Thus, you should be skeptical about putting money into a firm whose principals can't state their purpose in words you can understand.

In Keys 21–36 we discuss in general how to analyze a company's strength. Now let's apply some of what we learned specifically to high-tech stocks.

As in any business, good management is crucial to the success of a high-tech firm. Make sure the company's managers have experience in the industry and were successful in their last job. It is crucial to check out the credentials of those associated with the company. Fraudulent firms have been known to list an impressive array of consultants and connections they don't have. For example, according to the Pennsylvania Securities Commission, in 1987 the brokers at one firm falsely told customers that Dr. Frank Duffy of the Harvard Medical School was involved in a company called Applied Genetics. In another instance, a member of Congress discovered that he had been falsely listed as a member of the board of directors of Medical Dispensing Systems Inc.

Once you've decided that a firm's managers are who they say they are, you still have to determine whether they are capable of building a successful enterprise. Inadequate financial management and marketing are frequent problems for high-tech firms, which are often started by technical wizards with little experience actually running a business. Every company that intends to produce and sell something should have

49

these three areas of management covered: production, marketing, and finance. Often it's cheaper for a small, developing company to farm out the actual manufacturing of its product to an outside supplier.

An adequate supply of capital is also crucial to the success of high-tech firms, which generally need a great deal of money up front for research and development. It may take years for a company to develop a salable product, and you need to evaluate whether or not the firm will have enough resources to stay afloat until its idea comes to fruition. Venture capitalists who invest in such companies assume they will have to provide additional infusions of cash. Likewise, chances are good that high-tech firms that go public will need to raise more money later through additional stock offerings.

Even if a company's product sounds esoteric, you can still make a common sense judgment about whether you think there is a market for it. Once you've decided a product would sell, you should look at the competition. Some competition can be favorable: It shows that your company isn't the only one that thinks there is a market for some new gadget. But if another firm already holds a dominant position, a small upstart could have considerable trouble competing, especially in a business where the cost of entry is high.

Even if its product is similar to that of its competitors, make sure your firm offers customers some new twist, something they need, such as an added feature, greater convenience, or lower cost.

Be cautious about investing in a company that has thrown all its resources into developing a single product. The firm may not be able to sustain itself if sales for that product falter.

17

NATURAL RESOURCES

As noted in Key 16, mining and energy stocks no longer play a dominating role in the penny stock market. Nevertheless, they are important because of their historical significance and because another boom in energy or precious metals prices could make them all the rage again, encouraging new drilling and digging.

The wild, frontier quality of the penny stock market dates back to its birthplace in the gold and silver mines of the 1800s. In the 1940s and 50s, worthless shares in uranium mine stocks were bought and sold over the counter of a Salt Lake City coffee shop.

The mining scam is perhaps as old as mining itself. *De Re Metallica,* a mining treatise published in 1556, warned investors: "A prudent owner, before he buys shares, ought to go to the mine and carefully examine the nature of the vein. For it is very important that he should be on his guard lest fraudulent sellers of shares should deceive him." Some recent penny stock frauds have involved gold. The SEC recently suspended trading in the stock of Goldcor, a company that claimed to have 50 machines that could extract gold from the sands of Costa Rica.

Investing in mining and energy stocks is thus an extremely risky endeavor. When considering such an investment, you should hire a geologist to read the prospectus or, if you can afford it, examine the site where the mining or drilling is supposedly going to take place. A competent geologist should be able to tell right away if something in the prospectus is seriously amiss, such as a claim that the promoters are mining both gold and platinum in the same place when in fact gold and platinum are rarely found together. Call the American Institute of Professional Geologists at (303) 431-0831 to obtain a list of the geologists working in your area.

18

MANUFACTURING

Manufacturing is a broad category that includes everything from machine tools to computer chips. Many companies classified as "high technology" also would fall under the umbrella of manufacturing, assuming they produced a tangible product.

One important question to ask when evaluating a firm that plans to manufacture something is how much money the company has set aside to cover the cost of actually making and selling its product. High-tech companies are notorious for negligence in this area. Some venture capitalists say the selling price of a product should be four to five times what it costs to make, thus ensuring an adequate margin for the firm's marketing efforts and administrative costs.

You should also keep a sharp eye on your company's costs. One of the biggest problems American manufacturers have faced in recent years has been their high production costs compared with foreign, especially Asian, competitors. Entire industries, such as consumer electronics, have virtually disappeared from our shores. In response, U.S. companies have taken drastic steps to cut their own costs. Lean and mean were the bywords of the 1980s.

How can you tell whether or not a company will be able to survive in an increasingly competitive marketplace? If its product is something unique that can be found nowhere else, it stands a better chance of competing on the basis of that product alone. But if your company makes widgets similar to the widgets made everywhere else around the globe, it better have something else to offer, such as a unique service contract or a lower price. If the company is in an industry already dominated by large firms, it may have difficulty competing, because it won't have the clout to buy raw materials at a competitive price.

In order to avoid the expense associated with running a manufacturing operation, many small companies use their research to come up with a unique product and then hire an outside firm to assemble it. This can be an attractive method of containing costs and providing a company with flexibility, as long as the subcontractors are reliable.

When looking at the earnings and balance sheet of a manufacturer, keep close track of the firm's inventory level. A sudden build-up in inventory could mean that the company has overestimated demand for its product, while a sudden drain on inventory could mean that it has underestimated demand and will be caught short.

Also check to make sure that inventory is not rising substantially as a percentage of total sales. The high cost of keeping excess raw materials and finished products in inventory has led many American companies to adopt just-in-time delivery systems, under which they receive supplies and ship out finished products as shortly before they are needed as possible.

19

RETAIL

Within the retail sector there are many different subcategories, such as department stores, drugstore chains, sporting goods stores, and specialty apparel shops. All this variety makes general analysis difficult. For example, a healthy margin for a department store might not be a healthy margin for a specialty retailer. But there are some all-purpose tools we can use to measure a retailer's health.

One key indicator is the inventory turnover rate, which tells how quickly a firm can move its merchandise out the door. To obtain this rate, take the company's annual cost of goods sold and divide it by the average inventory level. For example, a company with an annual cost of goods sold of $10 million and an average inventory level of $2 million would have an inventory turnover rate of five.

$$\text{inventory turnover} = \frac{\text{cost of goods sold}}{\text{average inventory}}$$

What constitutes a healthy inventory turnover rate depends on the type of retailer you're looking at. To take one example, a strong drugstore chain may have a turnover rate ranging from five to eight. Compare the inventory turnover rate of your company with others in its industry to see how it stacks up.

We also want to be sure the company will be able to obtain adequate inventory in the future. Check to see that management has lines of credit in place. Also, the 10-K (Key 22) should include a discussion of any known problems on the horizon.

If a firm's inventory levels are rising, accounts payable should be going up, too. This indicates that the retailer probably has a good relationship with its vendors and is financing most of its purchases through them, avoiding the expense of taking out loans. If inventory is financed by long-term borrowing, however, it could mean the company is headed for trouble. Retail chains often expand rapidly. If your company is going through such a growth phase, check to make sure that administrative costs are not outstripping business growth. One way to do this is to determine the percentage of sales that operating costs represent. If this percentage is increasing, it may indicate that the firm is having trouble controlling operating expenses. Also, check to make sure that accounts receivable are not increasing at a rate faster than the company's in sales. There may be a collections problem.

One of the most important questions to ask when evaluating a retailer or for that matter, any company, is whether or not the firm's "idea"—the niche or product that is the basis of the business—has the potential for the growth needed to make your investment worthwhile. In other words, do you think it can fly higher and higher. You should also decide whether or not there is room for your company to capture a large share of the market. Suppose you were considering investing in a company that intended to sell gourmet cookie franchises. A good idea, but certainly not an original one. You'd need to consider whether or not your upstart firm had something different to offer that would allow it to compete.

20

STICK TO THE PROGRAM

The easiest type of company to follow is one involved in just one type of business, often referred to as a "pure play." When small companies stray into multiple businesses, caution is called for, as this example will illustrate:

In January 1984, investors in the initial public offering of Sportecular Inc., a Penfield, New York, retailer of ski equipment and bicycles, could have had little inkling of what lay ahead. They expected their money to be used to expand the moderately profitable chain of stores, and the prospectus didn't tell them any different.

But soon after the company went public, it acquired the assets of a radically different business: Target Vision Inc., a seller of closed-circuit information and message systems. Sportecular began pouring money into Target Vision, and saw its profits disappear. Finally, in the spring of 1989, Target Vision was taken over by its largest creditor—but not soon enough to prevent Sportecular from having to file for protection from creditors under Chapter 11 of the U.S. Bankruptcy Code.

Initially, most investors failed to see that Target Vision meant trouble for Sportecular. In fact, the stock leapt from $1.00 a share to more than $6.00 after the announcement. Even as losses mounted, Sportecular principals assured stockholders that profits were just around the corner. Unfortunately, the stock is now worth pennies. With the benefit of hindsight, analysts now say that Sportecular's entry into a different business in which its principals had no experience should have been a red flag to investors.

Sportecular's story is not unique. Often small companies flush with cash from a stock offering are tempted to make large acquisitions or to get into new businesses. Perhaps the new business looks to have more profit potential than the old business. Indeed, sometimes such investments work out well. In 1985 a company called Thoroughbreds USA went public as a penny stock, then changed its main focus from race tracks to movie making. The company went on to produce a moderately successful film, *Lady in White.*

In any case, when a company changes focus, it means you must reevaluate your investment because the company has strayed from the path it was on when you bought stock.

21

FINANCIAL DOCUMENTS

The most important step in searching out profitable penny stocks is learning where to find and how to interpret financial documents.

In this chapter we will start our 16-key look at financial documents.

This key tells what financial documents are available, what they contain, and where to get them. Subsequent keys will describe the various financial statements found in these documents and show you how to analyze them.

Because penny stocks are not followed by the research departments of large brokerage firms or standard research services, the task of getting hard information to launch a buying decision from will often rest with you. Fortunately, you have an ally in the federal government. A great deal of financial data and other information is on file with the Securities and Exchange Commission, and it is easily obtainable at little or no cost.

Form 10-K and the Annual Report. For a summary of a company's financial activities, including a description of the business, income statements (Keys 27–28), balance sheets (Keys 23–26), cash flow statements (Key 29), and an analysis of the numbers for the company's last fiscal year, get a 10-K document. A similar document is the annual report. But because an annual report isn't a required SEC filing, it may contain more, or less, or different information than does a 10-K.

Form 10-Q and the Quarterly Report. For a summary of a company's most recent fiscal quarter, including income statements, balance sheets, and cash flow statements, get a Form 10-Q. The 10-Q also includes other financial information as well as management's discussion of legal and any other problems.

Form 8-K. Any events or changes in a business that shareholders should know about are contained in an 8K statement, which must be filed within 15 days of the event.

Schedule 13-D. This document tells who owns more than 5% of a company's stock. If an individual or institution is accumulating a great deal of stock, it may signal a takeover.

Forms 3 and 4; Rule 144. These documents list trades by company insiders and intent to sell company stock by insiders, respectively. Insiders include officers and major stockholders. Because these people know the most about a company, their buying and selling of company stock is watched to predict good or bad fortune for the company. Generally speaking, then, insider buying of stock is a clearly good sign. However, selling may not be a bad sign; it depends on why the stock is being sold. Stock could be sold to raise money for extraordinary personal expenses, such as the purchase of a home. In other cases an officer might feel uncomfortable having all his personal wealth invested in one place. What counts in insider activity is the overall pattern of sales and purchases.

The Prospectus. This document contains most of the information listed above plus additional information of importance, such as a realistic appraisal of the outlook for the company's business. The prospectus is discussed in detail in the next key.

Obtaining Reports and Other Documents. The first step is to call the company directly. Many firms have someone designated to handle investor relations who can provide you with these documents. Or ask your broker for the information. If the broker is selling the stock, he or she should have this information handy.

You can also write to the Securities and Exchange Commission, 450 Fifth St. N.W., Washington, D.C. 20549, Attention: Public Reference Branch. You must specify which documents you want, state that you will pay the cost (currently 20 cents per page), and allow three to four weeks for delivery.

Private contractors also can provide SEC documents. Bechtel Information Services, for instance, can send documents on file first class or by express mail usually the same day you call them. Bechtel can be reached at (800) 231-DATA. Other document retrieval services include Disclosure Inc., (800) 638-8241. In 1990, Bechtel charged $26 for a 10-K, $17 for an annual report, $18 for a prospectus, $11 for a 10-Q, $16 for a 13-D, and $13 for an 8-K. Additional charges may apply.

22

THE PROSPECTUS

Before a company's initial public offering (IPO) of stock, it must first file a prospectus, which includes a detailed company history, financial information, biographical information on company officers, and cautions about the business. By law, this document must be available to prospective investors before a stock sale takes place—and for good reason. The SEC requires that the prospectus include not only all essential information, but also every conceivable warning to the investor.

Investors' first look at a company often comes from a preliminary prospectus, called a red herring because portions of the cover are printed in red ink. The red herring typically doesn't contain all the information in the final prospectus, and the information it does have may be revised.

What to look for. Unscrupulous brokers fear the prospectus, which is why you must read it. That's easier said than done. Whole books have been written on how to read prospectuses, which, like most legal documents, are written by lawyers for other lawyers. Nevertheless, you can learn how to get the information you need without undue strain. First, penny stock investors should study these four sections in particular; risk factors, management, use of proceeds, and dilution. (To look for specific sections, refer to the index on the back page.)

Because the key to penny stock investing is reducing risk, read risk factors carefully. The risk factors also act as a kind of second index for the prospectus, summarizing special risks and referring the reader to other sections that explore company risk in greater detail. Some risk factors are generic. For instance, all penny stock prospectuses contain the sentence: "The securities being offered hereby are speculative in nature, involve a high degree of risk, and should be purchased only by persons who can afford to lose their entire investment." That's true, but what you want to know about are the specific risk factors related to the company you're analyzing.

The most basic risk factor is this: Do the people running the company know what they're doing? That's not difficult to figure out. What would you think of a toy maker that said, "Management has no prior experience in the acquisition, development, manufacture and marketing of toys"?

Another risk factor is the strength of the company's competition. If there are well-established competitors with bigger marketing organizations and better financing, the new company had better have a unique angle to develop its business. (Thus, if you choose to look at this prospectus because you like the business the company is in, why not invest in its competitors?)

Also, the prospectus states that "These securities have not been approved or disapproved by the Securities and Exchange Commission." Do not make the mistake of many unsophisticated investors of assuming that the mere fact a prospectus exists connotes any seal of approval from the U.S. government. Should a company want to sell stock to build a rocket ship and explore the planet Pluto, the SEC would allow a prospectus.

Following is an examination of some prospectus sections.

Use of Proceeds describes the company plans in dollars and cents. One way to think of your company is as an unlit fire—wood and tinder that have been carefully arranged to leap into flame at the touch of a spark. In the ideal penny stock situation, use of proceeds from an initial offering should be that spark.

The money should be going to specific areas that will make the business grow, such as research and development, an advertising campaign, or acquiring other businesses in its field.

Be wary when a large part or all of an initial offering is going to pay off debt. The company may have dug itself into a hole, having made no real progress developing its product or service. All your money will be doing is bailing it out to try again.

Take the actual case of two small restaurant companies that wanted to franchise themselves. One had lost substantial sums before going public, was still losing money, and was planning to use up to 70% of money raised to pay off different types of debt. The other was making money—proving it already had a winning formula—and wanted to use almost all of its cash from a stock sale to develop a franchise program. At this writing, the debt-laden company is bankrupt, and the other has just signed its tenth franchise.

The rule here is: Invest in future results, not past mistakes.

Management is often a black-and-white issue. Do the people who will run the company have a good track record in the business? And if they are new to the business, have they had success in any other business? Will they devote all or most of their time to developing the business?

Some managers have used the penny stock market

as a money machine, raising money for different projects that they spend only a fraction of their time on and paying themselves a salary for each project. A sweet deal for them, but not for you. Remember, you're paying for a legitimate shot at big success, not indulging someone else's business fantasies.

Especially in companies with no business operations yet, be sure to check the salaries of company officers. Do salaries match their experience and education? Some officers have simply banked the proceeds from a multimillion-dollar offering and lived off the interest while half-heartedly trying to develop the business.

The qualifications of the board of directors members can also foreshadow a company's success or failure. Do the directors have experience relevant to the business, or are they simply cronies or relatives of company officers?

Dilution, simply put, is how big a bang investors will get for their buck. Dilution also shows how much money company managers have at stake. Human nature tells us the more managers are risking of their own money, the harder they'll work. In the worst case, investors put up almost all the money and yet will own a small percent of the company. This chart from a prospectus illustrates such a situation:

	Shares Purchased	Total Funds Invested	% of Total	Average Price Per Share
Previous Investors	30,000,000	$ 30,000	2	$.001
New Investors	15,000,000	$1,500,000	98	$ .10

Previous investors have put up only 2% of the money raised, yet will see their investment increase 100 times if the company's stock price is 10 cents per share.

At best, the company managers have already invested a great deal of money in company assets, and are truly trading a portion of these assets for some funding and a piece of their business, such as is illustrated by the following chart:

	Shares Purchased	Total Funds Invested	% of Total	Average Price Per Share
Previous Investors	4,500,000	$1,000,000	25	$0.22
New Investors	3,000,000	$3,000,000	75	$1.00

The rule here is that heavy dilution is a key warning signal. Management had better be bringing something very attractive to the table—such as experience, key patents, or a strong business plan—to justify heavy dilution, or else the new investors are being taken.

23

ASSETS

The balance sheet offers a look at a company's assets, liabilities, and stockholders equity at a certain point in time. It is called a balance sheet because the asset side must equal the sum of the liabilities and stockholders equity:

$$\text{Assets} = \text{Liabilities} + \text{Stockholders' Equity}$$

This equation holds true because every corporate financial entity appears on both sides of the balance sheet. So a new building appears as an asset under "property plant and equipment," while the mortgage on the building appears as a long-term liability. A stock offering increases both stockholders' equity and some category of assets.

By examining the balance sheet together with the income statement and cash flow statement, a penny stock investor can calculate if a company has the resources to develop its business plan, or if it's on the verge of collapse. In this and the next two keys we will examine the major components of the balance sheet, then in Key 26 we will show balance sheet examples.

67

Current Assets. Assets are listed from the most liquid—meaning the asset most readily converted to cash—to the least liquid. Here's a breakdown of what are called current assets on a typical balance sheet:

Cash. Some cash is essential to pay day-to-day expenses, but excess cash held for a long time is a waste. If the management of the penny stock company you have invested in also heads other companies with surpluses of cash, be suspicious. Some managers have been known simply to do several stock offerings and bank the money, not developing the business.

Marketable Securities. These generally are U.S. government Treasury bills or bonds, high-quality corporate bonds, or high-quality stocks—not penny stocks. A warning bell should go off if assets include penny stock from another company. Sometimes stock is transferred from one company to another to boost a balance sheet or for other dubious reasons. Because of the volatility of the penny stock market, those assets could evaporate tomorrow, severely damaging the company's financial health.

Accounts Receivable. Credit is often given to a firm's customers. This credit is expected to be paid within a month or two, and is counted as asset.

Inventory. Finished products or the components of finished products are counted as inventory. Be careful of a firm that has a high inventory in relation to its sales. Its products may not be selling well.

Prepaid Expenses. Money that has been paid (possibly to a supplier), but hasn't been used yet to generate income.

Fixed Assets. The next section of the balance sheet include tangible assets with longer lives, such as land, buildings, furniture and equipment. These assets are valued at what they cost the company to buy them initially, minus an accounting charge that is supposed to reflect how the assets are being used up. (See depletion, amortization, and depreciation in Key 27.)

Thus, a company's fixed assets may be over- or

undervalued. For example, ten years ago a company may have paid $1 million for an office building that is actually worth more today than it was when purchased. In such a case, because the property is listed at cost, the firm's assets are undervalued. Another firm may have paid $1 million for equipment that is now obsolete, hence worthless. Yet it may not have been written off, and thus be on the books as a $1 million asset.

Other Assets. Assets that don't fit the short-term and long-term asset description are lumped into an "other assets" category on a balance sheet. Of these, intangible assets need the closest scrutiny. Intangible assets often take the form of rights, granted to or bought by a company, that aid its business. Many penny stock firms' balance sheets contain substantial intangible assets, because the business depends on capitalizing upon them for success:

Patents grant the exclusive right to make, sell, or use a product or process, and last for 17 years in the United States.

Copyrights give exclusive control to the creator of a literary, musical or artistic work. They last for the life of the author, plus 50 years.

Trademarks and Trade Names identify a product or company and can last indefinitely.

Franchises are the right to sell a product or service under a trade name and generally have a 40-year limit.

Purchased Goodwill. When a company pays more than the net asset value when buying another company, the difference between the net asset value and price paid is entered as goodwill on the balance sheet. Presumably the acquiring company is getting more than inventory, equipment, and other assets to justify the premium. It might be getting the acquired company's good reputation, for example.

Research and Development Costs. In a developmental company, a great deal of money may have been sunk into developing new products. Because the knowledge acquired in R&D presumably will have a future value, it is counted as an asset.

The key to interpreting intangible assets is not to accept them at face value. Question their quality. For instance, a patent is worthless if no salable products can be built from it. Likewise, R&D costs may have been wasted money if they won't result in increased sales. And purchased goodwill can be a red flag when it far exceeds the net asset value of the company bought, especially if that company didn't have a healthy business or a good reputation when purchased.

Here is the form the asset side of balance sheet may take:

ABC Corp.
BALANCE SHEET

| | December 31 | |
	1988	1989
Assets		
Current assets		
Cash	10,000	12,000
Marketable securities	20,000	25,000
Accounts receivable	40,000	52,000
Inventory	200,000	240,000
Prepaid expenses	12,000	14,000
Total current assets	282,000	343,000
Property, plant and equipment		
Cost	500,000	450,000
Less depreciation	50,000	50,000
	450,000	400,000
Other assets		
Prepaid rent	20,000	20,000
Patents	50,000	45,000
Goodwill	310,000	8,000
	80,000	73,000
Total assets	812,000	816,000

24

LIABILITIES

The next balance sheet category, liabilities, can be viewed by this equation.

$$\text{Liabilities} = \text{Assets} - \text{Stockholders' Equity}$$

Liabilities are simply what a company owes, whether it's a loan that doesn't have to be repaid for ten years or a bill due in a month. Like assets, liabilities are ranked with time in mind. For liabilities it is which debts are due soonest, or current liabilities, that appear first on a balance sheet. These include:

Current Liabilities.

Notes Payable usually includes short-term debt owed to banks, but can also mean such debt owed to individuals such as officers of the corporation. When such notes are owed to individuals, be sure to find out who the individuals are and why they loaned the company money.

Accounts Payable is the mirror image of the asset "accounts receivable," and shows money owed to pay for goods or services necessary to run a business.

Current Portion of Long-Term Debt is the amount of

principal due on long-term debt, just as a portion of your mortgage payment is principal.

Interest Payable is that money owed on short-term and long-term debt.

Unearned Revenue is created by customers who pay in advance. This revenue can't be counted as income until the product or service is delivered.

Tax and Other Withholdings include funds the company has withheld from employees or others but has not yet passed on to the federal or other government.

Income Taxes Payable represent funds that should be set aside to pay quarterly or other installments on the corporation's income tax due.

Long-Term Liabilities. These noncurrent liabilities represent debt that isn't due for at least a year. Typically, this debt finances mortgages on land, buildings, and some equipment. Thus, mortgages payable, bonds payable and other long-term obligations make up this category.

Here is an example of the liability portion of a balance sheet:

XYZ Corp.
BALANCE SHEET

	December 31	
	1988	1989

Liabilities

Current liabilities		
Notes payable	5,000	6,000
Accounts payable	20,000	25,000
Current portion of long-term debt	3,000	3,000
Interest payable	2,000	2,500
Tax and other withholdings	1,000	1,300
Total current liabilities	31,000	37,800
Long-term liabilities	50,000	47,000
(see note B)	81,000	84,800

In our example we deliberately have not broken down the components of long term debts, but instead have included a footnote "see note B." You will often come across footnotes in financial statements, and it is important to read each of them. While some footnotes simply elaborate on a line or explain something too complex to fit on a financial statement, some contain crucial information.

25

STOCKHOLDERS' EQUITY

Whatever amount is left over after liabilities have been subtracted from assets is stockholders' equity, also called *net worth* and *net assets*. This figure represents the accountant's tally of the value of the stockholders' stake in the company.

It is important to realize that there is no bank vault where stockholders' equity is held. It is simply the estimated amount that would be left over for stockholders should the company be liquidated and all the creditors paid off. Remember, stockholders are paid off *after* all creditors. Losses are first absorbed by stockholders through a loss in equity.

Stockholders' equity can come from several sources. In many penny stock companies, especially young ones, the only source of stockholders' equity is money from a stock offering. For instance, if ABC Corporation raised $1 million in a stock offering, borrowed $1 million, and had a net loss of $100,000 in its first year of operation, assets would equal $1.9 million. From this amount the borrowed $1 million would be subtracted to get stockholders' equity:

$$\$1.9 \text{ million (assets)} - \$1 \text{ million (liabilities)} = \$900,000$$

If ABC Corporation had posted net income of $100,000, the equation would look like this:

$$\$2.1 \text{ million (assets)} - \$1 \text{ million (liabilities)} = \$1.1 \text{ million in S.E.}$$

While creditors get first crack at assets, their stake is limited to the amount of money they loaned the company. Stockholders, on the other hand, benefit as the business grows. Their equity is typically increased when the company's net income is kept in the company—called retained earnings—and not paid out in dividends. Penny stocks (or any stocks with a high degree of risk) almost never pay dividends because any earnings must be retained to help the business grow.

The stockholders' equity portion of a balance sheet typically contains the following:

Common stock. The value of common stock is listed at "par value," which is an arbitrary figure. Penny stock par values usually are a penny, or less, per share. Par value has no relation to market value.

Additional paid-in capital is the money received by the company from a stock offering in excess of par value.

Preferred stock is more like very long-term debt than common stock. Preferred stockholders are guaranteed a dividend, which usually must be paid before common stockholders receive a dividend. Like other creditors, preferred stockholders come before common stockholders when a company is liquidated. Also, in cumulative preferred stock, any dividend payments that are missed accumulate as liabilities, and must be paid before common stockholders can receive dividends. Preferred stock does not have voting rights.

Penny stock companies generally do not issue preferred stock, and any that do should be viewed with suspicion. The effect of preferred stock is to add another layer of risk to common stockholders' holdings.

Treasury stock represents shares that once were issued as common stock but have been bought back by the company and are held by the corporate treasurer.

When liabilities exceed assets, a company owes more than it owns—this is called negative net worth. Be wary of investing in a company with negative net worth. Unless the firm owns some terrific technology it has yet to capitalize on or is just about to turn the corner into profitability, steer clear.

26

BALANCE SHEET ANALYSIS

Now that we've examined the three components of a balance sheet, it should be obvious what a strong balance sheet looks like. Ways of testing the strength of a balance sheet are examined in Keys 31 and 33.

It is a fact that many penny stock companies do not come with strong balance sheets. Take the case of Hospitality Hostess Ltd., a "professional welcoming service." This company's representatives called on community newcomers to inform them about certain products or services in the community. Hospitality Hostess's revenues came from businesses that paid to have their products advertised in this manner.

As of the end of 1985, this company was in poor financial shape. The first clue can be found in the first line of the assets—the checking account owes $1,492. While the previous year's balance sheet would show that the total current assets have increased, they are still less than total current liabilities. This shows the company could have trouble paying its bills, because the money to pay bills—current assets—is less than

Hospitality Hostess, Ltd.
BALANCE SHEET
December 31, 1985

Assets

Current assets:

Cash—Checking	$(1,492)
Cash—Money market	40,821
Accounts receivable	20,840
Total current assets	60,169

Fixed assets:

Automobile	7,206
Furniture & fixtures	10,622
Leasehold improvements	304
	18,132
Less: Accumulated depreciation	10,813
Net fixed assets	7,319

Other assets:

Trade exchange receivable	1,637
Deferred offering costs	31,782
Purchased intangibles	65,000
Accumulated amortization	(28,167)
Noncompete agreement—net of amortization	51,652
Loan origination fees—net of amortization	600
Organization expenses—net of amortization	1,667
Prepaid commission	1,197
Total other assets	125,368
Total assets	$192,856

Liabilities and Shareholders' Equity

Current liabilities:

Accounts payable	$13,150
Accrued payroll taxes	1,323
Deferred revenue	29,997
Interest payable	875
Note payable—credit union	4,060
Note payable—bank	19,200
Noncompete agreement	15,534
Note payable—individual	2,000

Long-term debt:

Note payable—credit union	0
Note payable—bank	77,585
Noncompete agreement	36,118

Note payable—individual	4,000
Total long-term debt	117,703
Total liabilities	203,842
Shareholders' equity:	
Common Stock, $.0001 par value;	
authorized 100,000,000 shares	
Issued and outstanding	
31,200,000 shares	3,120
Capital contributed in excess of par	
or stated value	102,080
Retained earnings (deficit)	(114,866)
Less: Cost of Treasury stock	
(113,200,000) shares	(1,320)
Total shareholders' equity	(10,986)
Total liabilities and shareholders' equity	$192,856

the amount of those bills. (See Key 31.)

Next, note that "purchased intangibles" and "noncompete agreement–net of amortization" make up a major portion of the company's assets. As stated earlier, many penny stock balance sheets have large "intangible" line items that must be thoroughly explored. In this case, both items reflect money owed the company's previous owners to buy the business. A logical question to ask is, Was the price paid for the business a fair one? Will payments on that purchase put a heavy strain on the company in the future?

Skipping to the shareholders' equity section, we see that there are negative retained earnings. And while stockholders' equity is a relatively small negative $10,986, it would be ten times as large were it not for the "contributed capital" invested into the company. Retained earnings are a negative $114,866.

Despite this poor balance sheet (and a similarly poor income statement), Hospitality Hostess successfully went public—a tribute to the salesmanship of the underwriter.

Of course, many penny stock companies have few assets before going public, or may only have large sums of cash for a long time after going public, making their balance sheets very simple. For example, here's the initial balance sheet of International Consumer Brands Inc., a company that succeeded:

International Consumer Brands Inc.
BALANCE SHEET
July 31, 1985

Assets

Current assets:		
Cash	$398,671	
Prepaid expenses and other	11,239	
Total current assets		$409,910
Furniture and Equipment—At cost		
Net of accumulated depreciation		7,830
Other assets:		
Prepaid registration costs	12,500	
Deposits	3,313	15,813
		$433,553

Liabilities and Shareholders' Equity

Current liabilities:		
Notes payable	$50,000	
Accrued taxes and expenses	10,011	
Total current liabilities		$60,011
Shareholders' equity		
Preferred stock—no par value— authorized, issued and outstanding 1,000 shares	1,000	
Common stock, .01 par value— authorized 10,000,000 shares, issued and outstanding 2,480,000 shares	24,800	
Capital in excess of par value	389,200	
Deficit accumulated during development stage	(41,458)	373,542
		$433,533

27

INCOME STATEMENT

It may sound obvious, but making money is what public companies are all about. Increasing sales, hiring good people, attracting investors, and having sound plans for the future are some of the ingredients necessary for a business to succeed. But even when the best ingredients are mixed, a company still may not make money.

A company's stock price is pegged to the company's future ability to show profits. Profits, called net earnings or net income, are found at the bottom of a company's income statement—arguably the most important of the financial statements. Income statements summarize company revenues and expenses over a period of time, generally a year or a quarter (three months). Here is an example of a simplified income statement:

XYZ Co. Inc.
STATEMENT OF INCOME

Net sales	$100,000
Cost of goods sold	50,000
Gross profit	50,000
Selling, general and administrative expenses	35,000
Interest expense (income)	3,000
Earnings before taxes and extraordinary items	12,000
Income taxes	4,000
Earnings before extraordinary items	8,000
Extraordinary items (use of tax-loss carryforwards)	4,000
Net earnings	$12,000

Earnings per share before extraordinary items	$.08
Earnings per share	$.12

Net sales, the first line of the income statement, simply refers to the money the company has received or will receive for goods or services already purchased. It is called *net* sales because the amount is actually gross sales minus returns and discounts.

Cost of goods sold is the price the company paid for the tangible goods it sold. For example, a pizza parlor's costs would include flour, cheese, and pepperoni. For a service firm, of course, there is no cost of goods sold.

Gross profit is the net sales minus the cost of goods sold. Here, too, a service firm would not have an entry on this line.

Selling, general and administrative expenses vary widely depending on what the firm does, but include expenses such as salaries, advertising, employee benefits, paper clips, etc.

Few companies give more detailed views of these types of expenses, though an important component of them can be found in the statement of cash flows (Key 29). Noncash expenses include depreciation, amortization, and depletion.

Here's an example of depreciation: If a company buys an office building, for instance, it must write-off a portion of the building's price against income for many years. That depreciation expense isn't being put into a special fund to buy a new building, so no cash is being spent. It is simply an accounting exercise, and may or may not reflect the loss in value of the building. In fact, the building may be increasing in value.

When it's not a long-term asset, such as a building, being used up, but a natural resource, the write-off is called *depletion*. Oil, coal, gas or a mineral such as copper are depleted as they are taken from the ground.

Amortization writes off the value of a limited-life or intangible asset, such as goodwill. For instance, when one company buys another for more than the company's net asset value (assets minus liabilities), the difference is added to the balance sheet as "goodwill."

Interest expense is an example of an income statement category called "other expenses"—expenses not directly related to operations. This could simply be a long-term bank loan.

Interest income would fall in a category called "other income." As well as earning interest from investments, an example of "other income" could be the rent from a property owned by the company.

Notice that interest income, while it adds to net earnings, is added in *after* gross profits from the firm's business are calculated. This is because interest income should not be confused with a firm's income from its business operations.

A common mistake made by novices examining developmental stage companies is to skip to the bottom line. Because a young company that recently went public is rich in cash, by simply investing in bank certificates of deposits or U.S. Treasury bills, the company can often make a profit. This profit has no bearing on the company's future or its management expertise.

Earnings before taxes and extraordinary items is also called pretax income from continuing operations.

Income taxes. No explanation necessary.

Earnings before extraordinary items. Until now, we have been dealing with income and expenses that are expected to reoccur. This income statement line clearly separates those usual entries from unusual entries that are not expected to reoccur.

Extraordinary items could be loss of property from a tidal wave. For our example we have chosen use of tax loss carryforwards because this is an item that frequently occurs in growth companies that have just turned the corner into profitability. The government basically allows a tax break in recognition and compensation of past losses. In our example, the companies earnings are, in effect, totally sheltered from income taxes.

Net earnings is the bottom line and takes into account both ordinary and extraordinary entries.

Earnings per share before extraordinary items is simply the earnings before extraordinary items divided by the number of shares. In our example, the company had 100,000 shares outstanding.

Earnings per share are simply net earnings divided by the number of shares.

Income statements can be deceiving if income coming from the sale of securities is a major portion of profits. Small companies have been known to team up with brokerage houses to sell stocks at a profit, then use that profit to bolster the bottom line. Then both the company and the brokerage house that took it public are made to look good. Just as with interest income, this type of paper transaction has no relevance when it comes to developing the company's business.

Every financial statement must be viewed in context, and this is particularly true with young companies. Many young companies pour all their resources into increasing sales at the expense of profits to gain market share. So it is not necessarily a bad thing if profitability is still somewhere on the horizon, and the income statement shows a loss. This does not mean you should ignore the income statement of an unprofitable company—it is still loaded with valuable information.

28

INCOME STATEMENT ANALYSIS

To further our look at income statements, we will examine an established, profitable company; a company just becoming profitable; and a true developmental stage company. At the top of the next page is the income statement for The Village Green Bookstore Inc., a book, gift and stationery store.

In a retail firm such as Village Green Bookstore, the income statement is straightforward. The company buys its goods from other companies, sells them and lists that figure as sales.

A single income statement is useful, but by far the greatest worth of income statements comes when they are compared. This includes both comparisons between two periods of the same company, and also between companies. When comparing between companies, we generally use relative measures, such as percentages or ratios (Keys 31–34). For instance, we might observe that The Village Green's gross profit is

The Village Green Bookstore Inc.
STATEMENT OF INCOME
For the years ended Jan. 31, 1986 and 1985

	1986	1985
Sales	$2,844,830	$2,811,672
Cost of goods sold		
Beginning inventory	671,935	598,563
Purchases	1,949,866	1,976,211
Freight	40,747	32,623
Cost of goods available for sale	2,662,548	2,607,397
Less: Ending inventory	749,525	671,935
Cost of goods sold	1,913,023	1,935,462
Gross profit	931,807	876,210
Less: Selling, admin. and other expenses	863,149	817,682
Income before other income and taxes	68,658	58,528
Interest income	722	2,049
Income before income taxes	69,380	60,577
Income taxes	18,935	14,075
Net income	50,445	46,502

33% of sales. Similar companies may have much lower gross profit margins, showing that The Village Green is being run efficiently. On the other hand, similar companies may have much higher gross profit margins, indicating mismanagement and room for improvement in The Village Green.

When comparing different periods in the same company first make sure the periods studied are comparable. A retailer such as The Village Green's fourth quarter (during the holiday season) would have much higher sales than its first quarter (during the winter lull). Radical differences between periods can alert investors to both good and bad trends.

Now let's take a closer look at The Village Green's income statement, this time comparing 1986 results with 1985 results. First check the entries we want to see increase. Sales have increased by about $33,000 and gross profit has increased by about $55,500. Both positive, but small, changes considering the company has almost $3 million in sales. Selling, administrative and general expenses have increased about $45,500, however, largely wiping out the increase in gross profit. At this stage in The Village Green's life—just before it is to go public—the company is showing it knows how to run its business profitably, but that profit is not large and the company is not growing quickly.

Now let us take a look at another type of company in another type of business. Moscom Corp. makes computer products that help companies monitor and control telephone costs.

Moscom Corporation and Subsidiary
CONSOLIDATED STATEMENTS
OF OPERATIONS
For the years ended Dec. 31, 1983 and 1984

	1984	1983
Sales	$5,020,664	$102,348
Costs and operating expenses		
Cost of sales	3,602,084	615,039
Engineering and software development	1,291,693	922,529
Selling, general and administrative	2,636,387	1,766,072
	7,530,164	3,303,640
Interest expense (income)	(113,750)	(433,740)
Income (loss) before income taxes and extraordinary items	(2,395,750)	(2,767,552)
Income taxes		
Extraordinary items	212,869	(900,000)
Net income (loss)	$(2,182,881)	$(3,667,552)

Moscom during the 1983–1984 period was a developmental stage company and illustrated some important trends penny stock investors should look for. While it was losing substantial amounts of money, its sales were growing rapidly, its cost of sales as a percentage of sales were decreasing rapidly and it was spending substantial money on research and development (engineering and software development.)

During the next quarter, Moscom turned the corner into profitability. This is reflected in its first quarter 1985 and 1984 income statements.

Moscom Corp.
Three months ended March 31

	1985	1984
Sales	$2,840,881	177,567
Costs and operating expenses		
Cost of sales	1,495,054	279,780
Engineering and software development	393,180	279,993
Selling, general and administrative	785,937	589,145
	2,674,171	1,148,918
Interest expense (income)	13,893	(73,102)
Income (loss) before income taxes and extraordinary items	152,817	(898,249)
Income taxes	67,000	—
Income (loss) before extraordinary items	85,817	(898,249)
Extraordinary items	67,000	212,869
Net income (loss)	$152,817	$(685,380)

Sales continue their strong increase, and selling, general and administrative expenses continue to be a smaller percentage of sales (even when compared to all of 1984). And even though Moscom has increased its research and development expenses, it has still made a profit.

In the case of both The Village Green and Moscom, investors had plenty of income statement numbers to study. However, many penny stock ventures offer income statements such as this one for International

Consumer Brands Inc., a company that was organized to design, make and sell electrical and rechargeable personal care products as well as kitchen and home-care appliances.

International Consumer Brands Inc.
STATEMENT OF OPERATIONS AND DEFICIT
For the Period June 5, 1985 through July 31, 1985

Revenues		
Interest income		$2,665
Costs and expenses		
General and administrative	$26,887	
Product development	16,840	
Interest expense	396	44,123
Net loss and deficit		(41,458)

Obviously, at this stage ICB is nothing more than a business plan. In such a case when no real income statements are available, the investor must look elsewhere (such as the prospectus, Key 22) for information on which to base an investment decision.

29

STATEMENT OF CASH FLOW

As important as income statements are, the cash flow statement is gaining popularity as the main tool for financial analysis.

Cash flow is simply how much money a company spends and where the money has gone, and how much money has been received from whom. One way to picture a cash flow statement is a checkbook ledger which lists bills paid and checks deposited. Cash flow statements explain why changes in assets and liabilities have occurred between periods.

Because penny stock investors must pay close scrutiny to how their money is being spent, cash flow is key. Cash flow often is a better measure of company health than earnings because earnings can be puffed up or hidden through accounting changes or other manipulations that don't reflect the true state of a company's business.

The use of depreciation is often used to show the flaws in income statements. Remember that depreciation (Key 27) is an expense for which no money actually leaves the company.

The first step in developing a cash flow statement is to take net income and add back the depreciation expense, and similar charges such as depletion and amortization. Earnings plus depreciation and other non-cash expenses are often referred to by the umbrella term "cash flow," and is a gross measure of how much cash a company generates from its core business. Obviously, a company can't last forever unless its core business makes money, so this is an important measure.

Investors attached to a company's dividend often make sure this type of cash flow is positive. Continued losses in this area may indicate the company will drop the dividend. If the minimum needed to keep the company's plant and equipment running (a figure management could tell you) is deducted from this cash flow figure, the result is the financial icing on the cake called "free cash flow." Companies can use this excess cash to buy back their own shares, acquire other companies, pay-off debt, or pay more dividends—all of which should benefit shareholders.

Cash flow is used in different ways for different types of companies:

- For start-up companies, cash flow and free cash flow usually are negative, because the company is burdened with low sales and heavy investment expenses necessary to build the business. Matching the cash being lost in a cash flow statement to the assets on hand to pay bills (such as proceeds from a stock offering) can accurately predict how the company can survive with no additional funding.
- Cash flow is particularly crucial in oil and gas, and real estate companies, whose net income is often depressed or eliminated by heavy depletion and depreciation allowances.

Here is a cash flow statement of a healthy company:

ABC Corp.
STATEMENT OF CASH FLOWS
For the year ended 19XX ($000)

Cash flows from operating activities	
Net Income	300
Depreciation	50
(Increase) in accounts receivable	(200)
(Increase) in inventory	(200)
Increase in accounts payable	75
Increase in accrued expenses	50
Increase in taxes payable	30
Increase in deferred taxes	15
Net cash flow from operating activities	120
Cash flow from investing activities	
Purchase of property	(200)
Proceeds from sales of equipment	20
Net cash from investing activities	(180)
Cash flows from financing activities	
Notes payable issued	50
Common stock issued	2200
Net financing cash flow	2250
Change in cash balance	2190
Beginning cash	100
Ending cash	2290

Like all such statements, the above is divided into three sections:

1. Cash flow from operating activities. This focuses on the short-term and day-to-day cash inflows and outflows. This portion of the cash flow statement is done in two ways. The "indirect method," shown here, is the most common and

adds or subtracts from net income. The "direct method" lists overall cash movements, such as "payments to suppliers" and "collections from customers." The end result is the same.

2. Cash flows from investing activities. A company's purchase and sale of property, plant or equipment—long-term assets, are reviewed here.

3. Cash flows from financing activities. Money raised through avenues such as borrowing, or debt and equity offerings, fall in this category. So do payments on debt or equity, such as dividends.

As with any financial statement, cash flow is most useful when many periods are compared. ABC Corp. would include its cash flow for the last several years in its latest statement.

By simply looking at one statement, however, we can see that the company has a positive cash flow from operating activities, even though it has lost cash through increased inventory and accounts receivable.

Proceeds from a stock sale have swelled its ending cash total. If ABC Corp. has lost money from operating activities, and had done so at an increasing rate over the last several periods, we would know the company was headed for trouble.

30

EARNINGS PER SHARE

When it comes to financial language, "earnings per share" is one of the most widely used phrases. Earnings per share is net income, after taxes, divided by the number of shares outstanding. The trick to earnings per share is that shares outstanding can vary.

Earnings per share is divided into the price per share to give the powerful and widely-used price-earnings ratio, so it is crucial that investors know how earnings per share is calculated.

When a company has nothing but common stock, and the number of those shares hasn't changed during a year, earnings per share is simple. Here's an example of ABC Corp.'s earnings per share:

$$\frac{\text{earnings}}{\text{number of shares}} = \frac{\$1,000,000}{10,000,000} = \$.10$$

Now suppose ABC Corp. has to pay dividends of $100,000 to preferred stock shareholders. Earnings per share will decrease:

$$\frac{\text{earnings}}{\text{number of shares}} = \frac{\$\ 900,000}{10,000,000} = \$.09$$

If ABC. Corp. had issued an additional 500,000 shares of stock two-thirds of the way through its fiscal year, earnings per share would again decrease and would have to be determined through a "weighted-average" calculation:

10,000,000 shares × ⅔ year	6,666,666
15,000,000 shares × ⅓ year	5,000,000
	11,666,666

$$\frac{\text{earnings}}{\text{number of shares}} = \frac{\$1,000,000}{11,666,666} = \$.087$$

Finally, earnings per share can be expressed as "primary" or "fully diluted." If a company has other securities that can be converted into shares of stock, such as warrants (Key 44) or some types of preferred stock, it helps to know the effect on earnings per share if those securities were converted into stock and raised the number of shares.

Remember that more shares means less earnings per share.

So let's say when ABC Corp. went public it issued a warrant for one share of stock with each of its 10,000,000 shares. Primary earnings per share would be the same as in our first example. Fully diluted earnings per share would be:

$$\frac{\text{Earnings}}{\text{number of shares}} = \frac{\$1,000,000}{20,000,000} = \$.05$$

Because many penny stocks issue warrants, it pays to keep dilution in mind. But also keep in mind that fully diluted earnings per share is a hypothetical case.

31

LIQUIDITY RATIOS

Because so many young companies operate on the edge of bankruptcy, one of the first things investors should check is whether the company is likely to be around just for the short term. This boils down to one question: does the company have enough available money (liquidity) to pay its short-term liabilities? Liquidity ratios help measure short-term staying power, and therefore are especially crucial when examining the balance sheets of low-priced stocks.

The current ratio measures this short-term bill-paying ability through comparing total current assets by total current liabilities.

$$\text{Current ratio} = \frac{\text{Current assets}}{\text{Current liabilities}}$$

In general, current assets should be at least twice current liabilities, though this varies with the type of business. Once again, the current ratio should be measured over several financial periods to gauge changes and stability.

Just because a current ratio of 2 is good, doesn't mean one of 4, 6 or more is even better. This may indicate the company has too much cash—cash which should be invested in ways other than a bank account to develop the business. Not only could this be a sign of too much caution, it may reflect simple mismanagement of assets.

Especially after a company goes public, it may be flush with cash and exhibit a huge current ratio. This should not be a cause for concern.

Another, more stringent, liquidity ratio is called the quick ratio. The quick ratio compares current assets without inventories, to current liabilities.

$$\text{Quick ratio} = \frac{\text{Current assets} - \text{Inventories}}{\text{Current liabilities}}$$

The quick ratio is especially useful if the company is not having success selling its products, for whatever reason. If the inventories are not being converted to cash quickly, they may not be a dependable source for paying current liabilities.

A quick ratio of 1 is usually considered adequate.

32

PROFITABILITY RATIOS

Profitability means much more than a company's profit margin. Companies also must be evaluated on how profits compare with assets, stockholders equity and stock price. These ratios go straight to the heart of how well management is using company resources.

We'll start out by looking at the most familiar of these ratios: return on sales, commonly called the profit margin.

$$\text{Return on sales} = \frac{\text{Net income}}{\text{Sales}}$$

If Company X has net income of \$50,000 on sales of \$1 million, it has a return on sales of .05. To get a percentage, which is how profit margin is usually expressed, multiply by 100. This yields 5%.

Return on sales is an excellent measure of how efficiently a company is operating, especially when compared to previous periods and to companies in the same industry. Because many penny stock companies show no net income, investors may be tempted to dismiss profitability ratios, such as return on sales, as worthless. But there is value to substituting net loss for net income, and tracking the change over several periods.

Think of this measure as "loss on sales," and as the mirror image of return on sales. For instance, suppose our Company X has losses in consecutive years of: $30,000 on $100,000 in sales; $50,000 on $500,000 in sales; and $60,000 on $1 million in sales.

While losses have doubled in three years, the loss compared to sales has decreased dramatically, from 30% to 6%. Skyrocketing sales and decreasing losses as a percent of sales is an excellent trend for a penny stock company. If this trend continues, we can expect company X to soon break into profitability.

Return on assets measures how efficiently a company uses its assets.

$$\text{Return on assets} = \frac{\text{Net income}}{\text{Assets}}$$

If a company is in its development stages, and has a large amount of cash, a better return (or loss) on assets measure could be:

$$\frac{\text{Net income} - \text{interest income}}{\text{Assets} - \text{cash}}$$

This strips the consequences of a huge chunk of cash out of both the income statement and balance sheet, and allows for a better look at how the company is using its noncash assets.

Return on stockholders' equity compares income to the stockholders' investment in the company.

$$\text{Return on stockholders' equity} = \frac{\text{Net income}}{\text{Stockholders' equity}}$$

If there is preferred stock, the dividend to preferred stockholders is deducted from net income before this calculation is made. Also, stockholders' equity at the beginning and end of a fiscal period is sometimes averaged to get the denominator of this ratio.

The price/earnings ratio is another common measure of profitability.

$$\text{Price/earnings ratio} = \frac{\text{Price per share}}{\text{Earnings per share}}$$

Because this is crucial to pricing a company, this ratio is discussed in Keys 30 and 35.

33

LEVERAGE RATIOS

As we have often said in this book, minimizing risk is one of the most important keys to investing in penny stocks.

One way companies can increase their risk, but also increase their potential for great rewards, is through the use of leverage.

Leverage is simply long-term borrowing. In physics, the longer the lever the greater the weight that can be moved. In corporate finance, the greater the leverage the more assets that can be bought—assets which could bring more profits to a company.

The danger with leverage, of course, is what's borrowed must be paid back. If the business isn't successful enough, too great a debt load will sap company money and could cause financial problems or even bankruptcy.

Ratios that measure leverage can show trends in debt growth. When debt is high, investors must ask themselves if the company's future earnings will be enough to pay principal and interest on the debt.

The debt to stockholders' equity ratio is a leverage

ratio that gives perspective on the shareholders' stake in the company.

$$\text{Ratio of debt to stockholders' equity} = \frac{\text{Debt}}{\text{Stockholders' equity}}$$

If debt (total liabilities) is many times greater than stockholders' equity, that shows that debt holders have a much greater stake in company assets than stockholders. This would indicate a low margin of safety for shareholders—remember, debt holders get paid first in the case of liquidation.

$$\text{Debt ratio} = \frac{\text{Debt}}{\text{Assets}}$$

The greater the debt ratio, the greater the proportion of assets are owned by creditors.

The times interest earned ratio measures how well a company's earnings cover all its interest expenses. Stockholders want to see this ratio high to ensure the company can meet its interest obligations:

$$\text{Times interest earned ratio} = \frac{\text{Earnings before interest and taxes}}{\text{interest expense}}$$

Who holds the debt of a company is also a factor when determining the level of debt. Have company insiders lent the company money? Is it debt from a bank? Some penny stock investors like to see some bank debt, because it indicates someone with financial expertise has closely examined the company and is willing to risk a loan.

34

ACTIVITY RATIOS

Activity ratios measure how efficiently a company uses its assets.

For instance, inventory is an asset whose whole purpose is to be sold. When it sits on the shelf, it costs the company money; the quicker you sell inventory, the quicker you make a profit on it. If Company ABC keeps an average of $1,000 worth of inventory on hand, and had $10,000 in sales one year, that means it sold (or "turned over") its inventory ten times in that year.

$$\text{Inventory turnover} = \frac{\text{Cost of sales}}{\text{Average inventory}} = \frac{\$10,000}{\$1,000} = 10$$

Average inventory can be figured by adding the current period's inventory figure (on the balance sheet) with the last inventory figure and dividing by two.

Now suppose ABC sales jumped to $100,000 a year, and to meet deliveries efficiently ABC found it had to keep $5,000 worth of inventory on hand. Its inventory turnover has increased to 20.

$$\text{Inventory turnover} = \frac{\$100,000}{5,000} = 20$$

Seen another way, an inventory turnover of 10 means the average time it took to sell out the inventory was 36 days. (365 days in a year, divided by 10). As sales increased, the average turnover period dropped to about 18 days.

Accounts receivable are an asset which are more valuable the quicker they are collected. This is because the money collected can more quickly be put back to use in the company.

$$\text{Receivables turnover} = \frac{\text{Sales}}{\text{Average accounts receivable}}$$

We can divide by the receivables turnover ratio into 365 to find out how long it takes the company to collect on its receivables. If the company grants 30 days to its customers for payment, and the average age of receivables is well over 30 days, you know the company isn't collecting promptly. Or worse, some customers won't be paying at all.

Broader measures of asset use include the asset turnover ratio, which is often used to compare companies within the same industry:

$$\text{Asset turnover ratio} = \frac{\text{Sales}}{\text{Average assets}}$$

35

PRICE

Of all the factors to consider when buying penny stocks, the most important is price. A well-run company is no bargain if you pay twice what other investors would pay for it. And pricing tricks are often used to dupe unsophisticated investors. Don't be fooled like the man who walks into a pizza parlor and asks how many slices in a $10 pizza.

"Eight," says the cook.

"Gee, that's pretty expensive," says the customer.

"Well, what if I cut it into 16 pieces?" asks the cook.

"Now *that's* a bargain," says the customer. "I'll take two."

Just as the number of slices in a pizza is irrelevant to the value of the pizza, the price per share is irrelevant to the value of a company.

Why are stocks of young, risky companies so uniformly priced at below $5 a share? For a couple reasons: Low price sends a signal to investors that a stock is a speculative investment. The lower the stock price, generally the more speculative the investment, though there are many exceptions.

Also, there is the psychological reason used to fool investors, some of whom might think that having a *million* shares of stock worth a penny each is better than having just 100 shares worth $100 each. Don't let big numbers fool you. In actuality, both stakes add up to a $10,000 investment. Price per share is only useful when it is compared with other per-share information, such as dividends or earnings.

Especially with penny stocks, which often have no solid earnings or cash flow, the most important measure of a company's value is the price tag on the whole company, known as "market capitalization" or "market value." Market value is calculated by simply multiplying the number of shares of stock by the price per share. If Company A has 10 million shares selling for 10 cents each, its market value is $1 million. If the same company's shares sold for a penny each, the company's market value would be $100,000. If there's a healthy market for the stock, or if the brokerage house controlling the stock is honest, the market value should accurately reflect the value of the company. Market value can quickly alert you when a stock is priced outrageously or when it's a bargain.

One key to pricing a penny stock company is comparing the market value of the company with other companies in the same industry. Such comparisons can take many forms. First we'll examine general comparisons, then we'll examine comparisons using specific financial information.

Say an established, high-tech company in your city, Company A, has a market value of $20 million. It has a history of profits and is growing steadily. Now a penny stock broker calls and offers you stock in Company B, a developmental stage company with no profits and no growth record that also has a market value of $20 million. The choice between companies A and B would be like the choice between spending $1 million to buy a famous sculpture, and spending $1 million on a hunk of marble, hoping it would be carved into a work of art. A "sure thing" is much more valuable than a "could be."

The best comparisons can be made between companies in the same industry. For instance, compare an established chain of ice cream parlors, and a company that has only a business plan to open a chain of ice cream parlors and some money from a penny stock offering. Or a pharmaceutical firm that already has products on the market and Drugs 'R Us, that's still in the research and development stage. In both cases, the market value of the startup should be significantly less than the going concern. Yet, in many penny stock situations, the price of the firm is so far removed from reality that a start-up venture has a market value higher than established companies.

A valuable rule of thumb is that the longer you have to wait for the business to be a success, the less you should have to pay for it, because the future contains so much uncertainty and because a dollar today is worth more than a dollar a year from now.

Perhaps the most common way of pricing a stock is by comparing price with earnings. The price/earnings ratio (discussed in Key 30) offers a single number that is best used when comparing firms in the same industry. If a company you're investigating has earnings of 20 cents per share, and is in an industry with a P/E of 12, you know that $2.40 per share (.20 × 12/1) is a fair price for the stock. Less than $2.40 signals a possible bargain, more than $2.40 signals it could be over-priced.

The average price-earnings ratio for all stocks varies depending on the demand for stocks. When stocks are popular, the average P/E might be 20. In an average market, the P/E could be between 10 and 15.

Unless a firm's earning history is very consistent, the price-earnings ratio is best used when looking at projected earnings, not past earnings. Many factors can influence future earnings, such as new contracts, credit problems, loss of key employees, etc.

Because the P/E is a proportion, it is the same

whether it is calculated for the whole company or on a per-share basis. So a company with a market value of $10 million and earnings of $1 million would have a P/E of 10 ($10 million/$1 million). If the same company had 10 million shares of stock outstanding, it would have earnings per share of 10 cents, a share price of $1, and an earnings per share of 10 ($1/$.10).

So if you had two similar restaurant chains, Ice Cream Palace with a P/E of 15 and Ice Cream to Go with a P/E of 10, the better bargain would be Ice Cream to Go. However, if Ice Cream Palace had earnings growth much faster than Ice Cream to Go, the higher P/E could be justified.

So a high P/E can be a sign that a firm is poised for growth. But as with all ratios, caution is advised. A P/E can be high not just because the stock price is high, but because the earnings are low. Another way of looking at P/E is instead of dividing the price by the earnings, divide the earnings by the price, which gives a stock's *earnings yield.* So a stock with a price of $12 per share and earnings of $1 per share would have a P/E of 12, and a yield of 8.3 percent (1/12).

Many investors have an easier time grasping a yield, because it is the same type of measure used to judge other common investments, such as certificates of deposit.

Cash flow (Key 29) is another popular way of evaluating price and is used in much the same way as earnings. Simply multiply a firm's cash flow (usually cash flow from operations) by an industry multiple to come up with price. If you're considering buying into such ventures, at the very least look at several of them and buy the cheapest.

Aside from earnings, book value is also a common way to price a company and can be a good indicator when a company is underpriced. For instance, if you own stock in a company with a market value of $10 million, but has a book value of $20 million, the company has assets worth twice what stockholders are paying for them. Companies in certain types of industries trade at a "discount" to their book value—meaning less than their book value—while others trade at a "multiple" of book value.

The price-sales ratio (Key 32) compares one year of a company's sales to its market value. Generally speaking, when the market value equals the sales, the company is well priced, though sales exceeding market value by three or four times could still be justified if the company is growing rapidly.

The problem, of course, is that many penny stocks have no earnings from operations, little cash flow, and a book value that is either nonexistent or is mainly cash from a penny stock offering. Accurate pricing is impossible. These stocks trade at a price set by the enthusiasm of investors for management, the type of business they are in and the salesmanship (or lack thereof) of brokers dealing in the stock.

Perhaps the best rule-of-thumb for the market value of such companies came from the president of low-price stock firm that had taken many companies public. He said, "$5 million to $10 million is ball park for a startup company. Anything over that and you'd better give me a good reason, or it's just absurd." This contrasts with a penny stock broker, who tried to justify that the high market capitalization of many penny stocks because the companies may turn out to be the next Xerox.

A young company may become a huge success, but the odds of that happening are so slim. And because of those odds, high market capitalizations are not justified.

36

PRESENT VALUE

For investors not afraid of arithmetic, there are some calculations for estimating what a successful penny stock of the future might be worth today.

At best, they are inexact formulas for determining what a current stock price should be. However, they do get investors thinking about the price they pay for tying up their money in stocks, and what the company's risk level should do to the price of stocks.

The first formula takes into account that a dollar today is worth more than a dollar a year from now. This is because in the intervening year our dollar could be earning interest.

Let's say that we figure our stock will be worth an extra $1,000 at the end of two years. And if we didn't invest in the stock we could put our money in a nice, safe bank account earning an interest rate of 7 percent. (Rate = .07) To find the present value of that price appreciation, we would use this equation:

$$\text{Present value} = \frac{\text{Appreciation}}{(1 + R)^2} = \frac{\$1,000}{(1 + .07)^2} = \$873$$

Remember that ^{2} means "squared," (1.07×1.07).

Now let's assume that we won't be getting that appreciation for three years. Simply substitute a "3" for the "2" in our formula.

$$\text{Present value} = \frac{\text{Appreciation}}{(1 + R)^3} = \frac{\$1,000}{(1 + .07)^3} = \$816$$

The point is that the further away our reward is, the less it is worth to us today. So be particularly wary of companies that will take a long time to develop.

We can use present value to price a company that is expected to have a certain level of future earnings. Let's assume a company we're investigating has 10 cents per share in earnings at the end of two years, and is in an industry with a price/earnings ratio of 20. Today, we should be willing to pay about $2 for each share of stock ($.10 \times 20/1$). But what if the company tells us earnings won't start for two years?

$$\text{Present value} = \frac{\text{Earnings} \times \text{P/E}}{(1 + R)^2} = \frac{.10 \times 20/1}{(1 + .07)^2} = \$1.75$$

At this point, our formula assumes that 10 cents a share two years from now is a sure thing. Let's add one more twist to take into account that our company may or may not be successful. Suppose we determine it has a 50 percent chance of making it, or a probability of .50. Our formula becomes:

$$\text{Present value} = \frac{\text{Earnings} \times \text{P/E} \times \text{probability}}{(1 + R)^2} =$$

$$\frac{.10 \times 20/1 \times .50}{(1 + .07)^2} = \$.87$$

Such calculations help you choose among different investments, and also prove two important points:
- The more time until your reward comes, the less it is worth to you.
- The riskier the company, the less you should pay for it.

37

CASE 1: ROADWAY MOTOR PLAZAS

Now that we've reviewed the fundamentals of investing, we'll apply what we've learned to a real situation. For the sake of simplicity, the company we'll examine is in an easy-to-understand and an easy-to-analyze business—truckstops.

It's the fall of 1986, and a broker calls you with what he says is a hot deal. Roadway Motor Plazas Inc., a chain of seven truckstops in New York and New Jersey, is about to go public. Truckstops aren't the most exciting business, but as a smart investor you know that even a mundane business can be a good investment—as long as it's well run and the stock is sold at the right price. So you ask the broker to mail you a prospectus. When it arrives, you turn to the income statement to see if the company is profitable. Examining the figures (see next page), you find that Roadway is indeed profitable. What's more, profits increased 20.8% between 1985 and 1986. But sales are about flat, so you can't expect that kind of increase every year. On the other hand, with an offering price

Roadway Motor Plazas Inc.
INCOME STATEMENT

| | Year ended April 30. | |
	1986	1985
Net sales and operating revenues	$45,948,507	$46,143,448
Cost of goods sold	34,535,760	35,344,599
Gross profit	11,412,747	10,798,849
Operating expenses	9,426,817	8,939,921
General and administrative expense	443,911	437,753
Interest expense	310,262	461,034
Other income, net	(128,433)	(78,656)
	10,052,557	9,760,052
Income before income taxes	1,360,190	1,038,797
Provision for taxes on income	718,000	507,339
Net income	$642,190	$531,458
Earnings per share	$.21	$.17

of $2 per share, the current price/earnings ratio is just under 10. (More about this later.)

Next you look at cash flow from operations, just to double check that the net income is no illusion. You find "Net cash provided from operations" rose from $897,838 in 1985 to $1,124,614 in 1986. A healthy sign.

Next, look at the balance sheet (on the next page). Since only one year is given, you can't identify trends.

Because bill-paying ability is so important, the first ratio we'll look at is the current ratio (Key 31):

$$\frac{\text{Current assets}}{\text{Current liabilities}} = \frac{\$4,155,176}{\$3,382,883} = 1.22$$

Roadway falls short of our desired current ratio of 2. On the other hand, this is an established, profitable business, worth further investigation. To make sure the company is sound, look at a broader measure of financial health, debt to total assets (Key 33):

$$\frac{\text{Debt}}{\text{Assets}} = \frac{\$6,153,681}{\$7,799,697} = .79$$

114

Roadway Motor Plazas Inc.
BALANCE SHEET
April 30, 1986

Assets

Current assets:

Cash	$ 435,370
Short-term investments	725,908
Accounts receivable	1,470,060
Notes due from officers and directors	98,563
Inventories	1,154,317
Prepaid and other current assets	270,958
Total	$4,155,176
Property, plant and equipment	3,392,752
Other assets	251,769
	$7,799,697

Liabilities and Shareholders' Equity

Current liabilities:

Current portion of long-term debt and capital lease obligation	$ 406,742
Accounts payable	1,184,911
Accounts payable—affiliate	334,883
Accrued compensation	350,997
Accrued sales and fuel tax	621,083
Accrued expenses and other current liabilities	123,073
Income taxes payable	361,194
Total	3,382,883
Long-term debt and capital lease obligation	2,552,539
Deferred income taxes	156,400
Other long-term liabilities	61,859
Total liabilities	6,153,681

Commitments and contingencies
Shareholders' equity:

Convertible preferred stock, $.01 par value— 1,000 shares authorized, no shares issued	
Common stock, $.01 par value— 10,000,000 shares authorized and 3,120,000 shares issued and outstanding	31,200
Additional paid-in-capital	238,564
Retained earnings	1,376,252
Total shareholders' equity	1,646,016
	$7,799,697

So debts equal .79, or 79% of assets. Seen another way, shareholders' equity (the cushion between debt and assets), equals 21% of assets. This $1,646,016 represents a healthy piece of stability for the company.

So by many measures, this is a stable company. The next question is, how efficiently is the company operating? Here's where profitability ratios come into play.

$$\text{Return on assets} = \frac{\text{Net income}}{\text{Total assets}} = \frac{\$642,190}{\$7,799,697} = 8.2\%$$

An ROA of 8.2% doesn't seem like much, especially when you can receive a similar return from a bank certificate of deposit, federally insured. But by using return on assets with net income *before* taxes, you can see the company has an ROA of 17.4%. That's quite a bit better.

$$\text{Return on equity} = \frac{\text{Net income}}{\text{Owners' equity}} = \frac{\$1,360,190}{\$1,646,016} = .82 \ (82\%)$$

Another healthy sign.

Much more can be done with the financial statements, especially when it comes to comparing Roadway with similar companies. But this cursory look tells us the company is increasing in profitability, using its assets well, and is stable.

Other parts of the prospectus show us that the management is seasoned and has a history of success in the same or similar businesses. Furthermore, the company plans to use most of the proceeds from the public offering to buy or build more truck stops. This is reassuring, because you want a company to stick to what it knows best.

At this point you may be getting ready to call the broker and invest in the company.

Wait. You have two more key points to check out: Is the stock selling for a fair price? Is the underwriter reputable?

First, the price. The dilution section of the prospectus shows us that the book value per share before the company goes public is 53 cents per share. New investors will contribute 46 cents per share in book value, making the book value after the stock offering 99 cents per share. Remember, shares are being sold for $2 per share. The logical question is, do truckstop and similar companies generally trade at more than their book value? It turns out they do, so $2 per share is very reasonable based on book value.

After the company goes public, it will have 5,120,000 shares outstanding, giving it earnings per share (Key 30) of about 13 cents based on 1986's net income figure.

$$\frac{\text{Earnings}}{\text{Number of shares}} = \frac{642,190}{5,120,000} = 12.5 \text{ cents per share}$$

With that figure, we can calculate a price/earnings ratio:

$$\frac{\text{Price}}{\text{earnings}} = \frac{\$2.00}{\$.125} = 16$$

A P/E of 16 is reasonable—perhaps a bit high depending on market conditions. But remember, this P/E has been figured using *last* year's earnings. If the offering is successful, the company will have over $3 million it presumably will use to increase earnings.

Seen in that light, the P/E looks cheap and Roadway looks to be an excellent buy. Now, in the next key, we will examine if the broker is reputable.

38

CASE 2: THOMAS JAMES ASSOCIATES

Based on the analysis contained in Key 37, you decide Roadway Motor Plazas is a stable company being offered at a reasonable price. Once again, you are tempted to reach for the phone. But there's one more thing to consider.

Roadway's merits alone won't determine what happens to the price of its stock. Another, almost equally important factor, is the track record of the brokerage firm or firms underwriting the shares. In the penny stock market, the underwriter's ability to market the shares successfully can play an enormous role in the success of the underwriting and the stock's price in the aftermarket.

The underwriter in Roadway's case is Thomas James Associates, a Rochester, N.Y., brokerage firm. Roadway's prospectus says Thomas James has agreed to handle the company's 2-million-share offering on a *firm commitment* basis, which means that Thomas James will buy the shares itself and then sell them to investors, thus guaranteeing that Roadway will sell all 2 million shares. This type of underwriting is somewhat less risky for investors than one done on a *best efforts* basis, in which the underwriter pledges to do its best to sell all the stock but makes no guarantees.

Now the question is whether or not Thomas James has the wherewithal to find enough investors to buy Roadway stock. If not, the brokerage firm will have to keep some of the stock itself, and the price will likely drop after the offering. So you ask for a history of the brokerage and the stock offerings it has attempted.

Thomas James was just a little over a year old when it offered Roadway's stock to the public, but it already had completed five underwritings (one just a few days before Roadway). Most of these firms were less financially solid than Roadway, so there was little chance that Thomas James wouldn't be able to sell Roadway's comparatively attractive stock to its customers.

The next question you must ask is how well the other stocks brought public by Thomas James have performed. In order to do this, you compare the price at which they came public to their current price (when Roadway went public in September 1986). This process is complicated by the fact that many penny stock offerings are done in units of common stock and warrants to buy stock, which trade separately once the offering is completed. Roadway is the first stock offering Thomas James did that didn't involve warrants.

On the next page is a chart summarizing the history of Thomas James's completed offerings at the time it was taking Roadway public. The offering prices are given in units, but the September 1986 prices reflect the value of individual shares of common stock.

Judging from these numbers, you decide that Thomas James's offerings have done pretty well; all but one is trading above its offering price. But these stocks haven't been on the market for very long, and

Company Name	Date stock went public	Price per unit	Price per share of common stock in Sept. 1986
Zab's Backyard Hots Inc.	April 1985	$1/unit (unit contained 1 share, 1 warrant)	$1.75
Digicom Communications	Sept. 1985	$1.50/unit (3 shares, 2 warrants)	12.5 cents
International Consumer Brands	Dec. 1985	$1/unit (1 share, 1 warrant)	$2.375
Anodyne Energy	Aug. 1986	$1.50/unit (3 shares, 1 warrant)	62.5 cents
Videospection	Sept. 1986 (came public 3 days before Roadway)	$2 unit (4 shares 1 warrant)	62.5 cents

new issues often do well initially only to drop later. Indeed, all of Thomas James's stocks at one point traded substantially higher than their offering price, a fact some critics say had more to do with the brokerage's sales force than with the companies' merits.

One thing you couldn't have known in 1986 was that three of these stocks would be worthless by 1989. And only one—International Consumer Brands—would be trading well above its offering price.

Nevertheless, your investment in Roadway Motor Plazas would have paid off. By mid-1989, Roadway was trading at $3.625, well above its offering price of $2 but down from its high of $6.38 in August 1987. Faced with this track record, you need to ask yourself what enabled Roadway to sustain its value over time when most of Thomas James's stocks didn't.

It all comes back to the financial soundness of Roadway itself. Through its sales efforts, a brokerage firm can support the price of a stock in the short term, but it is unlikely to keep finding buyers if a company keeps turning in poor financial results each quarter. A stock's price eventually will reflect the underlying company's worth. In Roadway's case, the company's sound fundamentals attracted other brokerage firms to trade its shares, and by 1989 a liquid market had developed.

On the other hand, the first company Thomas James underwrote, Zab's Backyard Hots Inc., a hot dog stand franchiser, was in Chapter 11 bankruptcy, its stock worthless. How could an investor have predicted that Roadway would succeed while Zab's would flounder? Let's look for clues in Zab's income statement and balance sheet at the time it went public in April 1985.

Zab's Backyard Hots Inc.
INCOME STATEMENT

	1984	1983
Sales	$1,527,387	$1,088,686
Cost of sales	524,946	365,289
Gross profit	1,002,441	723,397
Operating expenses	1,111,318	641,746
Restaurant closings	107,150	
General and administrative expenses	887,416	478,750
Total expenses	2,105,884	1,120,496
Loss from operations	(1,103,443)	(397,099)
Other income (expense)	(54,813)	8,161
Net loss	($1,158,256)	($388,938)

Unlike Roadway Motor Plazas, Zab's wasn't profitable. In fact, its losses increased almost 200% between 1983 and 1984. Meanwhile, sales rose just 40% while operating and general administrative expenses rose 78%.

Next, a look at Zab's consolidated balance sheet, where we find more red flags.

Zab's Backyard Hots Inc.

CONSOLIDATED BALANCE SHEET
Year ended Dec. 28, 1984

Assets

Current assets	$209,057
Property	614,458
Other assets	155,764
Total assets	$979,279

Liabilities and Shareholders' Equity

Current liabilities	$1,259,661
Long-term liabilities	112,102
Capitalized lease obligations	103,464
Shareholders' equity (deficiency)	(495,948)
Total	$979,279

Remember the current ratio, that key measure of bill-paying ability. Roadway Motor Plazas had a current ratio of 1.22, meaning that its current assets were 1.22 times its current liabilities. But Zab's current ratio is less than one: Its current liabilities are six times its current assets.

$$\frac{\text{Current assets}}{\text{Current liabilities}} = \frac{\$209,057}{\$1,259,661} = .16$$

All in all, it should have been no surprise when Zab's went "belly up."

39

CASE 3: STAR PUBLICATIONS

We've learned how to evaluate a company's chances for success by looking at the earnings statement, balance sheet, and other items contained in its prospectus. Now let's test our knowledge by looking at one case in which a company's prospectus and later SEC documents clearly contained the seeds of failure.

Star Publications Inc. of Denver, Colo., was a true penny stock: The company first offered 60 million shares of stock to the public in December 1986 at one cent for a unit that consisted of one share of common stock and one warrant to purchase stock.

Formed in November 1985, just one year before its public offering, the company purported in its prospectus to be a publisher of football annuals and game day athletic event programs. But by reading "The Company" section of the prospectus, the potential investor would have found that Star had published just one football annual, for the U.S. Air Force Academy, and no game-day publications. Despite this limited experience, it had the ambitious plan to publish annuals for 16 universities in the 1986 football season.

Another piece of disturbing information contained in this section of the prospectus was the disclosure that the schools would pay nothing for the annuals, that Star would make its money solely through the sale of advertising. Upon reading further, we find that Star has just two full-time employees.

Moreover, those who bought stock in Star's initial public offering would have immediately experienced a dilution of their investment as high as 82%, the "Dilution" section of the prospectus (Key 22) revealed. The company's existing shareholders would still control 66% of the stock though they had paid only $21,450 for their shares. In contrast, the new investors would control 34% of the firm with their investment of $600,000. According to Star's earnings statement (below), *gross* profit (before administrative expenses) was just $6,291. That means it cost the company almost as much to produce its first football annual as that publication earned in advertising dollars, and that was before employees got paid.

Star Publications Inc.
From Nov. 6, 1985 (inception) to July 31, 1986

Revenue:	
Advertising	$30,912
Consulting	481
Finance charges and interest	115
Total revenue:	$31,508
Publication costs	$25,217
Gross profit	$6,291
General and administrative costs	
Salaries	$31,000
Other	22,394
	$53,394
Net Loss	$47,103

Next let's look at Star's balance sheet:

Star Publications Inc.
BALANCE SHEET
July 31, 1986

Current Assets:	
Cash	$5,148
Accounts receivable	2,849
Employee advances	50
Prepaid interest	520
Total current assets	$8567
Equipment, net depreciation	3,591
Total assets	$12,158
Current liabilities:	
Accounts payable	$4,802
Accrued interest	3,874
Accrued salaries	8,900
Notes payable	21,370
Total current liabilities	$38,946
	(26,788)
	$12,158

Shareholder's equity is negative $26,788. A glance at current assets vs. current liabilities tells us Star Publications probably is in a cash crunch already.

$$\frac{\text{Current assets}}{\text{Current liabilities}} = \frac{\$8,567}{\$38,946} = .22$$

Add to Star's shaky balance sheet a footnote attached to its prospectus: "The continuation of the company is dependent upon obtaining the equity financing contemplated by the proposed public offering to meet working capital requirements." In other words, this company hasn't come close to making it on its own, and only a stock offering will keep it in business.

Surely, you say, nobody would invest in such a

dubious venture. But Star managed to sell 53.42 million units of its stock, more than the minimum required to complete the offering.

A year later, the company had published only one more annual, again for the Air Force Academy. It was unable to obtain enough advertising to complete the other 15 it had planned. Star's board suspended the publication of annuals in the summer of 1987.

The story only starts there, though. On February 10, 1988, Star, by then basically a worthless shell, merged with InnerVision Inc., a firm that claimed to hold the marketing rights to two types of disposable razors created in Italy.

The stock shot up to 16 cents after Power Securities Corp., a penny stock house that specialized in questionable deals, got into the act, setting loose more than 1,000 brokers to sell their clients on the potential of the folding "matchbox" razor, Star's primary product. Many investors bought the stock near its high price. They didn't know that the marketing rights to "matchbox" were the subject of a legal dispute. Indeed, in a September 1988 arbitration decision, the rights were awarded to a California firm. Of course, the stock price dropped like a rock. Investors could have known about this dispute ahead of time by reading the financial statements (Key 21) Star filed with the U.S. Securities and Exchange Commission.

The stock fell even further and had become virtually worthless when Power Securities closed in February 1989 under pressure from regulators. Power and Star were later named as defendants in a $1.035 billion class action suit brought by former investors. The outcome of that case was still pending as of fall 1989.

Clearly, investors who took the time to penetrate the hype surrounding Star Publications and discovered all the risks would have kept their checkbooks closed and saved money in the long run.

40

CASE 4:
ROCHESTER
VENTURE

It's May of 1986 and you've just received a cold call from a broker from a penny stock firm called American Heritage Securities. He is trying to sell you stock in a company called Rochester Venture.

Even before considering the merits, or lack thereof, of the company, a smart investor would have said "no thanks" for a number of reasons. A potential client asked about seeing a prospectus before buying the stock. The broker responded: "Before? Probably not. We're going to mail them out on Monday or Tuesday and it's already oversold. You'll get a prospectus and everything, but nine times out of ten people see a prospectus and they don't even buy it. Because, you know, it's written so people do get turned off by it. Because it is a speculative investment."

In those few words the broker said the client was being asked to buy stock in an underwriting that was already sold out and was told he couldn't see a prospectus before buying. Nevertheless, the potential customer persisted and asked if the company had any earnings yet.

"Ah, past earnings, I probably could get a hold of that later on. But that'll be in the prospectus when you get it. Those will be mailed out . . . in a couple days."

You can't hang up quickly enough on a broker with a pitch like this. Further investigation into the underwriting showed the company was not only shaky on a fundamental basis, but that the broker lied or twisted the truth repeatedly about Rochester Venture.

Rochester Venture, according to a preliminary prospectus, was a financial consulting firm which, at the time the stock was being sold, had one client, North Atlantic Fisheries. That business relationship was a close one: The president of Rochester Venture was the treasurer of North Atlantic Fisheries, a fact contained in the prospectus but not mentioned in the broker's sales pitch.

The prospectus also said that Rochester Venture planned to make money in the import-export business and by investing in other companies, though it had yet to do either of those things. However, the broker said Rochester Venture "had been around in the Rochester area for a while," having been incorporated "back in 1984. They're not a young start-up." The prospectus said "the company has had only limited operations for a very short period of time."

Rochester Venture, the broker said, "makes money by engaging primarily in the financial consulting business. They also have their hands in the import and export business and they also make money on the side by investing in other companies."

In fact, Rochester Venture had never made money investing in companies plural—just in one company. As far as having "their hands in the import and export business," the prospectus said: "The officers of the company have limited experience in the business of financial consulting and have not been involved in the import or export business."

The broker said he was "excited" about the stock for several reasons. American Heritage's underwriting track record was "flawless," with each of its three issues going up anywhere from "60 to 90 percent." And with the warrant included with shares of stock, "I don't see how we can miss."

It was true that all of American Heritage's underwritings had traded to a premium. However, the company hadn't been in business very long, so no long-term results were available. A look at the company's other underwritings would also have shown that none of them had any significant fundamental value, that the *same management* was involved in all of them, and that the companies were connected by owning each other's stock or loaning each other money. The steady influx of cash from the underwritings themselves seemed to be keeping the companies' alive, not the success of any of the individual businesses.

The idea that warrants can make the underwriting fail safe is ridiculous. This was especially true in the case of Rochester Venture, which was to be sold for 50 cents per unit. Each unit was to contain two shares of stock and a warrant which could be exercised for $1 up to two years after the offering was completed. So Rochester Venture stock would have had to quadruple in price for the warrant to be worth anything.

In spite of all these reasons not to buy Rochester Venture, the issue indeed was sold out. However, regulators prevented the company from ever going public, and several months later American Heritage Securities itself went out of business on the heels of fines and suspensions from regulators.

The price of stock in most of the companies it underwrote soon plummeted and never recovered.

41

BLIND POOLS AND SHELLS

A blind pool is a public company that doesn't tell stockholders where their money will be invested. Investors in blind pools tip-toe down the fine line between gullibility and faith.

Though the term *blind pool* is a blanket term for companies with uncertain futures, it specifically applies to stock offerings where investors know the general industry their money will be invested in when the blind pool first goes public. For instance, a blind pool may tell stockholders in the prospectus that management intends to invest in oil and gas or real estate. Once the blind pool raises money in an initial public offering, it acquires some assets and the blind pool's officers generally stay on to manage the acquisitions.

Blind pools differ from *blank check* companies, which give investors no clue at the initial offering what businesses they will invest in.

Both blind pools and blank checks can be thought of as "shell" companies, or empty public companies looking for businesses to acquire. The potential for abuses is obvious, ranging from the officers of the shell companies making poor investments to embezzling money from the shells. These officers also have been known to sit on the money invested, paying themselves a nice salary from interest earned. Or to invest in a company or companies that will enhance their own wallets, not those of stockholders. Or simply to walk away with investors' money.

Yet, during some years blind pools and blank checks have dominated penny stock new issues. During 1988, for example, these shell company offerings accounted for 70% of new issues, according to a Securities and Exchange Commission study. However, the study showed that the shells accounted for less than 1% of the money raised from new issues that year, with the average about $360,000.

Following a crackdown by state and federal authorities and the enactment of legislative restrictions by a number of states, the number of initial public offerings in the various types of shell companies had dropped dramatically by the end of 1989.

When properly and legally executed, blind pools and blank checks can bring quick profits to investors and quick cash and other benefits to the businesses they merge with. Here is one way a blank check company can work:

A financier and a brokerage house get together and raise $350,000 from the public for a company we'll call Blank Check Y. Remember, investors have no idea where the money will go, except in the most general terms.

The financier eventually finds an established business we'll call Company X, which wants to go public. Why would the president of Company X want to be acquired by, or merge with, a blank check? For three reasons.

First, going public has many advantages beyond

raising money in the initial offering of stock. Chief among them is raising more money from either warrants (Key 44) or a secondary offering of stock, or by acquiring other companies through stock swaps.

The second reason is timing. For a company to go public from scratch, it may take between 6 and 18 months to have the proper documents drawn up, the deal negotiated with the underwriter, and revisions on the prospectus made. Also, market conditions often change, so selling stock might not be worthwhile or even profitable months down the line. If Company X wants money now, wants stock for acquisitions or wants to take advantage of a "hot" market for stocks, half a year could be too long to wait. Going public through acquisition by a shell company can take as little as a month.

The third reason is cost. Most of the cost of going public has already been incurred by the blank check, and costs in general are reduced going the blank check route.

So Blank Check Y acquires Company X, creating Company XY. Most of the stock goes to the owners of Company X (after all, they have contributed most of the assets). The financier, realizing he has no expertise in running Company XY, but has just acted as a financial intermediary, bows out of the picture. His reward is company stock. And, of course, the shareholders in Blank Check Y have also received some stock in the merged company.

If the deal has been negotiated properly, the value of Company X's business has been matched to the number and price of the company's stock shares so that the stock immediately sees a large gain. If done improperly, investors could end up paying $1 share for assets worth a dime, so that eventually the value of Company XY's shares drops.

If you can find blank check underwriters that have a history of doing profitable deals, then you might find blank checks enticing. If they have no history or a poor history of acquiring good companies after money has been raised, your risk level will rise dramatically. This is also true for a blind pool company in which the management intends to invest in various businesses and then manage those assets. Does the management have a successful history in whatever industry it wants to invest in? Do those managers have other business interests that will distract them from running the company?

When checking the history of blind pool or blank check managers, make sure you look at the performance of shells at least a year *after* some businesses were acquired. Just because the stock price of the shell jumps initially doesn't mean it's a good long-term investment.

Another type of shell company is what's left over after a public company goes bust. Even though the business is gone, it is still a public company, which means it has some value. Financiers sometimes buy these companies and use them as blank checks. However, these companies sometimes contain the remnants of a defunct company, and defunct companies often leave disgruntled creditors or stockholders. For this reason it's important to look at shells very closely before buying into one.

Occasionally, shell companies will have large amounts of cash left over, either because money was never spent or from the liquidation of a business. Also possible is that cash on a per share basis will exceed the price per share. A $1 stock with $2 in cash per share can be a great buy, especially if you have confidence in company managers to acquire a valuable business. Or, management could liquidate the company and simply divide the proceeds among the shareholders.

42

INITIAL PUBLIC OFFERINGS

An initial public offering, or IPO, is a private company's first offering of stock to the public. Often, especially in the case of penny stocks, an IPO represents less of an opportunity for IPO investors than it does for those who invested before the IPO. This is due to two reasons. First, with dilution (Key 22), the value of these pre-IPO investors' stock can be greatly enhanced. Second, pre-IPO investors for the first time have an easy way to dispose of their stock—in the public market.

Stock bought in an IPO can rise quickly and substantially, often on the first day of trading. In the best case this rise is the result of the stock being sold at a bargain price to IPO investors. When the stock starts trading publicly, other investors recognize this bargain and want to buy the stock, even at a higher price.

The quick rise might also be due to market manipulation.

To invest wisely in any IPO, you should know how

the IPO process works. A company looking to raise money publicly can sell shares of stock itself, called a self-underwriting, or can shop for an investment banker to sell shares for it. The brokerage house has a sales force that sells shares to existing clients and potential clients, and for placing the stock it receives a portion of the total money raised, usually from 10% to 20%.

IPO stock can be sold in several ways: on a best efforts basis, through a firm commitment underwriting, and in a stand-by agreement. *Best efforts* means an investment banking firm has the option to buy stock and the authority to sell it, and they pledge to do their best to sell the stock. With a *firm commitment underwriting,* the investment banker buys all the shares in the offering and then resells them to the public. This is the preferred way to raise IPO money, because the company is guaranteed funding. *Stand-by agreements* are usually used in rights offerings (Key 44).

With a best efforts deal, a minimum number of shares must be sold for the IPO to go through. If this minimum is not sold, money is returned in full to those investors who put in orders to buy shares. While waiting to make the minimum, investors' money is placed in an escrow account. The investment banker has 90 days to make the minimum, and can receive a 30-day extension beyond that. Sometimes the investment banker in a best efforts deal is erroneously called an underwriter. Do not confuse the two.

The drawbacks to a best efforts IPO for an investor include the following:
- Because a company would prefer a firm commitment, a best efforts shows that no investment bankers were confident enough in the deal to underwrite it. So a best efforts signals that it is of particularly high risk or of particularly low interest to the investing public.

135

- Money can be tied up for four months and then returned—without interest—if the minimum is not reached.
- If only the minimum is reached, the company may not have raised enough money to develop its business plan. This means that another offering must be made, or more debt secured, if the company is to make a go of it. Both these alternatives add additional risk to the company.
- The risk of a best efforts deal not being completed is compounded when it is self-underwritten. Many companies feel they can sell their own stock, but using a professional sales force greatly increases the chances that enough stock will be sold.

Should you invest in IPOs? The short answer to that question is *yes* if you are a short-term investor and *maybe* if you are a long-term investor. Studies have shown that penny stock IPOs, on average, offer greater returns than stocks already on the market. However, the returns tend to be less predictable than those of the average stock. Less predictable, of course, means riskier.

Research indicates that initial returns tend to be greater in companies with less of a track record. Authors of an IPO study speculate that the reason for this is that very young companies are inherently riskier, so company owners must price their stock offerings especially low in order to entice investors to buy the shares. This may be true. However, some securities experts believe there may be other reasons, as follows:

- The price of these startup firms is more easily manipulated than the price of more established firms.
- Dishonest underwriters tend to like underwriting very young companies.

Remember that the investment banker who sells IPO stock has a vested interest in seeing the stock's price rise. Such a rise will not only attract other companies to use the investment banker for their underwritings, but will also entice shareholders to buy more stock through the investment banker.

Another study of penny stock IPOs concluded that while IPOs tend to be good deals in the short term, investors generally make no gains or even have losses after the stock has been trading over a month. Price volatility increases in this period, too.

"Unquestionably, if you were to take 1,000 IPOs that came public in any period of time, most of these stocks would be trading below their offering price," said Allan Hadhazy, senior analyst at the Fort Lauderdale–based *New Issues* newsletter.

A final caution: When an IPO is self-underwritten, the firm may take the attitude that once the stock is sold and it has its money, it no longer cares about the stock price. Such a firm may not actively seek market makers, and so the stock price might languish.

Unless you're investing for the short term, hoping to cash in on a quick rise in an IPO and then get out, make sure the IPO is being sold by an honest underwriter and will have good support after it starts trading.

Companies choose to go public for a variety of different reasons. Here are major classifications of companies and why they go public:

Startups. These are companies with no business operations whatsoever. Company managers hope to raise money through the sale of stock and use that money to start a business from scratch. Startups usually carry the highest degree of risk, especially if the managers have little or no experience in the business they want to start, or if the firm is in a highly competitive industry.

A typical startup might involve an entrepreneur who wants money to buy land to drill for natural gas. Or someone wants to start an import-export business. At the time they go public, these firms have almost no assets to their name. Why do they need to sell stock? Usually because no bank will lend them money, and they can't get financing any other way. The stock market is often the last resort for such companies.

Bridge Bets. Entrepreneurs often start a business with private financing, then find they haven't enough cash to last until the company becomes profitable. Or maybe they planned to go public while still developing their businesses. In any case, they need bridge financing to pay keep the company going until it can start paying for itself. Think of bridge bets as companies in a race with their ever-dwindling bank accounts.

Seedlings. These are small companies with a successful business already in place, but which need additional money. This money is often spent to pay off debt, to buy new equipment, or to develop a new product or service. For instance, a company manufacturing a new microchip may need money to build a new factory to improve production. On the other hand, sometimes a seedling will go public just to make money for company owners. When a company is private, it is often hard to sell ownership stakes. However, when it goes public through a sale of stock, the original owners can generally cash in on their ownership stake in the business.

Expanders. These are companies that have a winning formula for the business they're in, and think the business would be better if it were bigger. Expansion might mean developing a franchise program, so others can start identical businesses and pay the original company fees and percentages of profits. Or a company might want to buy other companies in the same business. Or a company may want to clone its business at new locations.

These companies may not have been particularly risky before they sell stock, but by raising money and aggressively pursing an expansion plan, they are taking risks.

43

STOCK SPLITS

A stock split, sometimes called a "split up," simply increases the number of shares outstanding in a company, normally with a corresponding decrease in price per share. For example, if you owned 100 shares of a $1 stock that split 2 for 1, you would end up with 200 shares of a 50-cent-per-share stock. Your holdings still would be valued at $100.

Another form of split is a *stock dividend.* The only difference between a split and a dividend is a difference in degree. While a split usually increases a stockholder's number of shares by 50%, 100%, or more, a stock dividend will typically yield the shareholder less than 25% in new shares. A 5% stock dividend will yield five shares for every 100 owned by the shareholder.

Why are stocks split? Typically, splits occur when a stock's price has become so high that it has a dampening effect on trading. This is linked to the fact that stocks usually are traded in blocks of 100, called round lots. Trading fractions of 100 shares often results in the broker charging a higher commission for the transaction. For example, if a stock reaches $200 per share, most investors would not want to spend $20,000 to buy a round lot. But after a 10 for 1 split, the price per share is lowered to $20, and the price of a round lot is just $2,000.

Some theories hold that a lower stock price will bring more investor interest. In addition, studies indicate that some companies time stock splits to coincide with favorable announcements, such as dividend increases. This research was not done on penny stocks, however. Because penny stocks will never, by definition, become so expensive that they require a split to decrease price per share, don't think that a split penny stock is any more valuable than a pre-split penny stock. In fact, if a broker or company leads you to believe a stock split is to your benefit, you should wonder if your trust in them is well-placed. This is especially true if a broker uses a split to entice you to buy more stock.

Another red flag is when, after a split—all things being equal—the stock price stays at the pre-split level. This would be a clear indication of price manipulation or the lack of a healthy market for the stock.

A *reverse split* decreases the number of shares, and so should increase the price per share, assuming the company's business is healthy and its stock is not overpriced. But sometimes a reverse split does not have the intended effect. For instance, several years ago there was a case where a new company had a chairman who didn't like his company's stock priced in the penny stock arena. The stock price was about $1 per share. He engineered a 1 for 5 reverse split, which should have raised his company's stock price to around $5 per share. However, it quickly sank down to $2.50 per share. Stock traders said that the company was still too speculative to be considered anything but a penny stock, and the market priced it down accordingly.

44

WARRANTS AND RIGHTS

Subscription warrants and subscription rights are legal claims to buy common stock issued by a corporation. Subscription warrants, better known simply as warrants, are usually issued with bonds or preferred stock, not common stock. However, the use of warrants is very common among penny stock companies.

Here's how warrants typically fit into a penny stock initial public offering: When you are offered stock in an IPO, often you are not simply offered shares of stock but "units," each unit consisting of a share of common stock and one or two warrants. For example, the stock may sell for 50 cents per share, and the warrant gives you the option to buy an additional share of stock at 60 cents per share (called the exercise price) by January 1 of next year (the exercise date) for each share you own.

The company is hoping the price of the stock will rise to say, 70 cents per share, making the exercise of the warrant for 60 cents a share result in an instant ten-cent-per-share profit for the warrant holder. In this case the company gets more money, and the stockholders get more stock at a bargain price.

Most warrants are negotiable, meaning they can be sold to someone else. For instance, in our example the warrant holder might not want to buy additional stock, so warrants might be sold to another investor for 5 cents each. The new warrant holder exercises the warrants and buys stock selling on the open market for 70 cents a share for the 60 cents each. The net cost is 65 cents (60 cents per share plus the 5-cent cost of the warrant.)

Warrants are prevalent among penny stocks because young companies often have a continuing need for more money to build their businesses. By adding warrants to an offering, the company virtually guarantees itself one or two new rounds of financing if their stock price rises. The key to warrants is to remember their nickname in the securities business: "sweeteners." While nice to have, they are only worthwhile if the stock price goes up.

Like most aspects of penny stocks, warrants have their downside. Suppose that after an IPO the stock price goes up due to market manipulation or hype. A warrant holder who has spent $1,000 in an IPO might be enticed into exercising some of his warrants and doubling his investment in an overpriced or worthless company.

If the company's stock shows signs of manipulation, or if you feel your stake in the company is high enough, the best strategy is simply to sell the warrants. If your broker has a great deal of trouble finding a buyer, watch out. That may signal there's no firm market for your stock, either. It may be a good time to sell. Also be wary if the price of your stock rises above the exercise price just before the exercise date. That may be a sign of price manipulation to get you to spend money and exercise your warrants.

A *subscription right* is a privilege granted to existing shareholders by a corporation wishing to sell more stock. Basically, it gives these shareholders a right to buy stock in a new issue before any stock is offered to the general public. As opposed to warrants, which may not expire for months, years, or even be perpetual, rights offerings generally expire after a few weeks or months. Otherwise, the two are basically the same. In fact, the actual document that is issued to shareholders in a rights offering is called a subscription warrant.

A right may give you the option to buy an additional share of stock for each share you own, or it might be in some ratio. For instance, for every 100 shares you own, you can buy 25.

For a rights offering to be worthwhile, the new shares must be offered significantly below the market price. If the stock's price takes a suspicious leap just before the rights offering, or if you don't want to increase your stake in the company, simply sell the rights.

Often rights offerings are sold using a standby agreement with an investment banker. Under such an agreement, the investment banker agrees to buy any shares not purchased in a rights offering for a fee.

A standby agreement works like an insurance policy for the company issuing rights. The risk of not raising a minimum amount of money in the offering is transferred to the investment banker, often called the standby underwriter.

45

STOCK CERTIFICATES

When investing in low-priced stocks, it's smart to get your stock certificates in hand, rather than leaving them registered in the "street name" of your brokerage house. If the shares are registered in your own name, the company you've invested in will send its quarterly, annual and special reports directly to you rather than to your broker. This ensures that you will receive such information in a timely fashion, as long as the company complies with SEC filing requirements.

Having your stock certificates will also allow you to more easily sell your shares when you want to and shop around for the best price, provided there is more than one market maker in your stock. The penny market is a negotiated one, and different brokerage houses sometimes offer widely differing prices.

If you run into difficulty selling your stock, having possession of your stock certificates will allow you to search for another broker. Such situations are not uncommon. The bid price supposedly being offered for your stock may suddenly disappear when you ask to place a sell order. Or your broker may say the market is not liquid enough to absorb the sale of your shares.

The compensation systems of some penny stock firms are set up to encourage brokers to urge customers to buy, buy, buy but never to sell. Some firms don't pay their brokers commission on sell orders. In some cases, brokers have to refund the commission on stock their customers bought if it is resold within a certain period of time.

And if your brokerage house should fold, not by any means an infrequent occurrence in the penny market, you may save valuable time by having your shares. Your stock ownership will be insured by the Securities Investors Protection Corp., but the value of that stock will not. You could lose an opportunity to sell while trying to obtain your stock certificates.

Your broker may resist sending you the certificates. As long as his firm has them, it controls your stock. Also, without possession of your stock certificates, the brokerage firm has no assurance that you won't take your business elsewhere. Don't let your broker dissuade you; insist on getting the certificates. If persuasion does not work, threaten to contact state or federal securities regulators and the National Association of Securities Dealers. If threats do not work, follow through on your threats and make sure you send copies of your letters to regulators to your broker.

46

ABUSES

The advice contained in previous chapters should help you pick the right broker and firm in the first place. But because many dishonest penny-stock outfits exist, you should monitor your account carefully to make sure it's being handled properly. These are some common forms of customer abuse:

Churning. When a broker trades excessively in a customer's account to generate commissions, he or she is churning the account. One way to judge whether your account is being churned is by calculating the annualized turnover rate, or ATR. To find the ATR, divide the number of shares you bought in the past year by the number of shares in your account. For example, if you bought 100,000 shares of stock this year but maintain only 20,000 shares in your account, your portfolio has an ATR of five. Generally speaking, an ATR of five means your account probably is being churned. An ATR of six presents clear evidence of churning. However, because commissions in the penny stock business are already high, an ATR as high as two could seriously damage the performance of your account.

Suitability. Perhaps the most common complaint among penny stock investors is that their broker exposed them to an unacceptable level of risk. It is the broker's responsibility to evaluate how much risk is proper for his or her client to take, but negligence of this duty has historically been difficult to prove. Keep in mind, it isn't in the broker's best interest for you to park your money in bank certificates of deposit. The riskier the investment, the higher the commission.

Unfortunately, the people who buy penny stocks too often are not experienced market players investing prudent amounts, but individuals who have never invested in the stock market before and are enticed by some fast-talking broker's promises of instant wealth. Too late, they realize it wasn't such a smart move to put all their savings in such risky stocks. These investors may receive some protection from new rules approved by the Securities and Exchange Commission in 1989.

The new rules require brokers putting new customers in low-priced "pink sheet" stocks to obtain prior written authorization. The brokerage firm must also keep in its files a written justification detailing why the investment is suitable for the customer and obtain a signed statement detailing a customer's financial situation and investment goals. The rules do not apply to stocks priced at more than $5 or listed on one of the exchanges or the National Association of Securities Dealers Automated Quotation System. Nor do they affect companies with more than $2 million in tangible net assets.

More experienced investors also are exempt. No written approval is needed from customers who have made three or more trades in any of the designated stocks in the past year, or who have maintained an account at the brokerage firm for more than one year.

Other abuses. Brokers have been known to abuse their clients in a variety of other ways, from ignoring their requests to sell stock to buying stock without their consent. When pitching stock, brokers sometimes omit important information or even tell lies about the companies they are promoting. Penny stock firms have been known to go so far as to create fictitious financial statements for their companies.

Another common and illegal form of abuse is charging customers undisclosed, excessive markups and markdowns on stock they buy and sell. Markups are described more fully in Key 11.

Here are some ways to protect your account from these and other forms of abuse:

- Keep detailed records. Retain copies of all mailings from your broker. Keep a log of the time, date, price and amount of all orders you place and compare it against your confirmation slip when it arrives.
- Confirm expensive and complex orders in writing, rather than over the phone.
- Ask your broker for a periodic total of all the commissions you have paid.
- Request that your broker keep you up to date on the value of your stocks.
- Call other brokerage houses from time to time and ask what price they show for your stock.
- Do not give your broker discretionary power over your account.

If a problem does arise, don't sweep it under the rug. For example, if your broker executes an unauthorized transaction, write him as soon as you receive your confirmation slip and demand that the trade be undone. If it isn't done in a reasonable amount of time, you may want to visit a lawyer to decide your next course of action. Sometimes, mere threats of legal action will cause a brokerage firm to settle up.

You can file a complaint against the broker and the firm with the National Association of Securities Dealers, the U.S. Securities and Exchange Commission and state securities regulators in your home state or the state in which the brokerage firm is based. Addresses for the SEC and NASD are listed below.

Normally, neither the SEC, the NASD nor state regulators will get you your money back, although they may discipline the firm or even force it to close. While it probably won't help your pocketbook, a complaint to regulators could prevent the same thing from happening to other investors.

Methods of seeking financial justice are described in the next two keys.

National Association of Securities Dealers
Surveillance Department
1735 K St., N.W.
Washington, D.C. 20006

Securities and Exchange Commission
Office of Consumer Affairs and Information Services
Mail Stop 2–6, 450 Fifth St., N.W.
Washington, D.C. 20549

47

ARBITRATION

If you feel that you have suffered financial losses because of wrongful behavior by your broker, and you want to take legal action, you have two options: arbitration or litigation (Key 48). Actually, you may have only one option. Whether you know it or not, you may have signed a document when you opened your account that agreed to bring any disputes to arbitration rather than going to court. Lawyers who represent investors in securities cases say many of their clients unknowingly sign such agreements.

Arbitration involves many elements of the judicial process: lawyers, expert witnesses, hearings, cross examinations. Cases are heard and decided by panels appointed by the organization administering the arbitration. The major financial exchanges, the NASD and the American Arbitration Association all operate arbitration panels that decide securities disputes.

The number of arbitration cases has ballooned in recent years, partly because of U.S. Supreme Court rulings that extended arbitration to violations of the anti-fraud provisions of federal securities law. In 1988, the NASD received 3,990 cases for arbitration, more than 12 times the 318 cases it received in 1980.

Arbitration is generally cheaper than going to court, but costs can still run into the thousands of dollars. And, in most cases, the loser has no right of appeal. Investor advocates say damage awards are usually smaller than those provided by the courts. Arbitrators rarely award punitive damages.

Many securities lawyers say the arbitration panels run by the NASD and the stock exchanges tend to be biased toward brokerage firms. Investors have had trouble obtaining documents, and the results of arbitration have often been kept secret.

In 1989 both the SEC and the NASD adopted rule changes to make the arbitration process more equitable for investors. One of the key changes requires brokerages to clearly highlight and explain agreements that bind investors to settle disputes through arbitration rather than the courts.

The new rules also require arbitrators to disclose their employment history for the previous ten years and to take other steps to disclose a potential pro-industry bias. Brokers will have to produce more documents. The results of arbitration cases will be made public.

Even with these reforms, investors have very little reason to sign an arbitration agreement when opening a brokerage account. As a member of the NASD (and/or a stock exchange) a brokerage firm already has bound itself to take disputes to arbitration. Therefore, by not agreeing to the arbitration portion of the customer agreement, the investor retains the right to go to arbitration or to file a lawsuit.

Some investor advocates say they get better treatment from arbitration panels operated by the American Arbitration Association than from those operated by the securities industry. If you do sign a pre-dispute arbitration agreement, you may want to designate that AAA will be the forum for any dispute.

In taking a case to arbitration or to court, it's important to move quickly once you realize you've been wronged. Even if your action is still allowed under state and federal statutes of limitations, delay will provide your opponent with legal ammunition. These favorite industry arguments all involve the investor's lack of swift action:

- By not objecting earlier the investor in effect agreed to accept the broker's action.
- The investor could have mitigated his losses by selling his stock sooner.

Despite the importance of a speedy response, investors often wait six months to a year before they even consider taking legal action. Some investors go through a denial stage in which they believe that bad luck, rather than any action by their broker, caused their losses. And, no matter how miffed, some investors will let themselves be placated over and over by their broker's pledges to remedy the situation.

For arbitration cases involving $50,000 or more, you'll want to hire a lawyer and perhaps an expert witness to testify in hearings on your case. Even in smaller cases, it would be wise to have an attorney review the written and oral arguments you plan to use. Remember, your opponent is sure to have the best counsel money can buy. When shopping around for an attorney, make sure you ask for one who specializes in securities litigation. Otherwise, your lawyer may charge you for the time it takes him or her to come up to speed on securities law.

Cases involving less than $10,000 in losses can use small claims arbitration, a simplified and less costly procedure in which a single arbitrator attempts to decide a case on written arguments rather than oral hearings. When bringing a case to arbitration, it is important that you prepare well for the hearing. Arrange for witnesses and evidence to be available for presentation. If the opposing side declines to produce documents voluntarily, your attorney and the arbitrators on the case have the power to issue subpoenas. If the arbitrators issue a subpoena, you still have the obligation of paying to have it served on the opposing party.

Once the arbitrators are appointed, check their backgrounds. Investors have complained that some arbitrators, while not technically part of the securities industry, are lawyers who often do work for securities firms. In arbitration run by the NASD, you have the right to ask that one arbitrator on the panel be replaced. You also have the right to ask that additional arbitrators be replaced if you have reason to believe they cannot give you a fair hearing. The arbitrator will be disqualified if your claim can be substantiated.

48

LITIGATION

If you decide to litigate your dispute, you'll most likely end up in federal court, because many complaints against brokers arise from alleged violations of federal securities law.

Federal court is generally a better environment than state court for investors in such cases, securities lawyers say, because it allows less opportunity for the brokerage firm to block the proceedings with appeals.

One thing to consider before taking the time and trouble of going to court is whether or not the brokerage firm will have enough money to pay damages if the court awards them to you. Many penny stock firms fold each year because of financial troubles or regulatory pressures, often leaving nothing behind. As the court process crawls along, any assets that were left may disappear.

Consider the case of Power Securities Corp. In February 1989, the same month the firm folded, a group of investors, alleging securities fraud, filed a $1.035 billion civil class action lawsuit against the brokerage, its principals and numerous other people who had been associated with the firm in some capacity. If the assets were out there, they were determined to find them. But by November 1989, almost a year later, the plaintiffs hadn't even been certified as a class by the judge.

If enough people have been wronged by your brokerage firm, the class action lawsuit can be a less expensive option than going to court by yourself. Lawyers sometimes will agree to pursue such cases on a contingency basis or for a partial fee up front to cover their costs. Nevertheless, the total cost of a class action suit can be prohibitive if the brokerage firm had thousands of customers, and your lawyers may not be able to drum up enough support among investors to pursue it.

Once again, consider the Power Securities case. The plaintiffs' lawyers estimate the firm may have had as many as 300,000 clients, all of whom would have to be notified of their inclusion in a class action suit. The cost of such notification, traditionally borne by the plaintiffs, would be prohibitive. As of this writing, the attorneys had asked the court to take the unusual step of requiring the defendants to cover these costs, or to redefine the class to a smaller group of investors who had contacted the law firm.

49

TURNAROUND SITUATIONS

Now that you are well-acquainted with the risks and rewards of penny stocks, you may decide that while you like taking risks, penny stocks are just a little bit too high for you on the risk pyramid (Key 5). But don't turn your back on all low-priced stocks.

There is a category of stocks that have two of penny stocks' criteria—low price and high risk—but lack the third. They aren't small companies. When you buy stock in an established company, you generally eliminate or reduce several of the risks inherent in penny stocks:

- You no longer have to gamble on whether the company has all the right ingredients to create a lasting business. It already has done so.
- You no longer must rely on just company projections and promises for future sales and earnings. You have plenty of historical data to look at.
- Perhaps most importantly, a large number of established, legitimate brokerage houses trade in established companies, so you can forgo background

checks on market makers. Because a healthy market already exists in these stocks, price manipulation, while possible, is highly unlikely.

How does an established company get a low price and high risk? Simple. It's in trouble. That trouble may be because a competitor has come out with a better product or a cheaper product. Or the company made a poor acquisition or spent too much money on a new product that nobody wants to buy.

In any case, that trouble is reflected in substantial losses or impending losses. Of course this causes stockholders, who bought shares thinking everything would be rosy, to sell, thus driving down the price.

Consider Computer Consoles Inc. This computer and communications company was started in 1968. Though its name may not be well-known, it had a healthy business. If you've ever called directory assistance, the recorded voice that read you the phone number probably came via a CCI computer. For years CCI's sales built steadily, and its stock—traded on the American Stock Exchange—topped $40 a share in the early 1980s. However, competition was stiff.

Between 1984 and 1985 its revenues dipped from $131.2 million to $111.9 million, while net income went from $6.3 million to a loss of $41.9 million. The company hired a new chairman in 1985, and he undertook a radical restructuring. By 1988 CCI was showing signs of a turnaround, though its stock price had dropped as low as $2.75 a share. The restructuring succeeded. And in December of 1988, with the stock trading at $8 a share, the company was bought by a British firm, STC Plc., for $12.80 a share. Investors who bought in the basement at $2.75 would have seen their shares increase 365% in less than a year.

Finding potential turnaround situations is easy. Because they are big companies, articles about them often appear in national newspapers and magazines.

50

FUTURE OF THE
PENNY STOCK
MARKET

In this book we've explored the potential rewards and plentiful risks of investing in penny stocks. We've seen that, on the one hand, the penny stock market provides a valuable means for small companies to raise cash and for investors to get in on those companies at the ground floor. On the other hand the penny stock market is also a mecca for crooked operators of get-rich-quick schemes. An investment in penny stocks is thus a high-risk investment. In the best of circumstances, where everyone involved is honest and above-board, young companies have a high failure rate.

Small investor complaints of penny stock fraud and abuse climbed 51% from 1987 to 1988, according to the North American Securities Administrators Association. That group has identified penny stock fraud as a major problem facing investors.

As this book goes to press, state and federal securities regulators are engaged in a campaign to clean up the penny stock industry. State securities agencies initiated 737 new investigations of penny stock firms in 1988, compared with 375 in 1987.

We believe low-priced stocks play a valid and useful role in society, but only when they are used for their legitimate purpose of providing funds for entrepreneurial ventures. America depends on small companies for much of its job growth and technological innovation, and the ability to issue stock can provide valuable capital for firms that might not otherwise be able to raise the money they need.

Because such companies will always be searching for funding sources, it's unlikely that the present crackdown will shut down the market for penny stocks. Hopefully, it will make it a safer, more profitable place for investors.

Some observers feel that regulatory pressures have acted to depress the prices of all low-priced stocks, which could mean that the early 1990s will be a good time to hunt for bargains in the markets.

The opportunities are there. We believe that those willing to do their own research by using the steps outlined in this book can still find good penny stock buys.

After all, the next IBM is bound to be out there somewhere.

RISK CHECKLIST

In Key 5 we touched on different types of risk to help put penny stock investing in perspective with other investments.

Now that we have explored the penny stock market, its analysis, and special situations in greater detail, we will return to risk to tie together all we have learned.

By filling out a checklist for each investment considered, you can be sure not to overlook key areas, and you can compare the risk/reward potential for all your investment candidates.

lower risk   higher risk

Broker risk

Brokerage firm underwriting the stock

established firm   young firm

☐ ☐ ☐ ☐   ☐   ☐ ☐ ☐ ☐

Regulatory Violations

few   many

☐ ☐ ☐ ☐   ☐   ☐ ☐ ☐ ☐

Sales tactics

low pressure   high pressure

☐ ☐ ☐ ☐   ☐   ☐ ☐ ☐ ☐

Investment products

Many products sold   Few products sold

☐ ☐ ☐ ☐   ☐   ☐ ☐ ☐ ☐

lower risk   # higher risk

(Price)

Low spread   high spread
☐ ☐ ☐ ☐   ☐   ☐ ☐ ☐ ☐

Low market capitalization   High market capitalization
(relative to company value)   (relative to company value)

☐ ☐ ☐ ☐   ☐   ☐ ☐ ☐ ☐

Steady price   Volatile price
☐ ☐ ☐ ☐   ☐   ☐ ☐ ☐ ☐

Many market makers   Few maker makers
☐ ☐ ☐ ☐   ☐   ☐ ☐ ☐ ☐

(The firm)

Experienced management   Inexperienced management
☐ ☐ ☐ ☐   ☐   ☐ ☐ ☐ ☐

Established business   Startup venture
☐ ☐ ☐ ☐   ☐   ☐ ☐ ☐ ☐

Few competitors   Many competitors
☐ ☐ ☐ ☐   ☐   ☐ ☐ ☐ ☐

Stable industry   Risky industry
☐ ☐ ☐ ☐   ☐   ☐ ☐ ☐ ☐

lower risk   # higher risk

(Financials)

Company profitable		Company unprofitable
☐ ☐ ☐ ☐	☐	☐ ☐ ☐ ☐

Profits consistent		Profits inconsistent
☐ ☐ ☐ ☐	☐	☐ ☐ ☐ ☐

Strong cash flow		Weak cash flow
☐ ☐ ☐ ☐	☐	☐ ☐ ☐ ☐

Low long-term debt		High long term debt
☐ ☐ ☐ ☐	☐	☐ ☐ ☐ ☐

Low short-term debt		High short-term debt
☐ ☐ ☐ ☐	☐	☐ ☐ ☐ ☐

High net worth		Low net worth
☐ ☐ ☐ ☐	☐	☐ ☐ ☐ ☐

Few intangible assets		Many intangible assets
☐ ☐ ☐ ☐	☐	☐ ☐ ☐ ☐

Short period until profitable		Long period until profitable
☐ ☐ ☐ ☐	☐	☐ ☐ ☐ ☐

QUESTIONS AND ANSWERS

Who should invest in penny stocks?

Penny stocks are best suited for people who enjoy playing the stock market and can afford to lose their investment.

How should I use this book?

Read this book before, not after, you invest in penny stocks. It will provide valuable tips on how to assess the potential of a stock and how to choose a broker.

It will tell you how to weed out the many unscrupulous penny stock brokers in your search for an investment adviser. If, unfortunately, you've already been the victim of penny stock fraud, this book will describe the forms of recourse available to you.

The chapters dealing with financial statements are best read with the prospectus of a company you're considering at your side. Then you can see how your firm stacks up using the various ratios that help measure a company's financial health.

What is a penny stock?

The answer to this question should be easy, but it isn't. There are at least three different definitions of penny stocks floating around: stocks priced under $1, stocks priced under $3 and stocks priced under $5.

For the purposes of this book, penny stocks are those priced under $5 and traded on the over-the-counter market, rather than on a stock exchange. Securities regulators generally don't include stocks listed on the National Association of Securities Dealers Automated Quotation System in their definition of penny stocks. But we are including NASDAQ over-the-counter stocks. There are approximately 4,330 companies listed on NASDAQ. Another 11,000 stocks are found only in the "pink sheets," a daily circular produced by a private firm. Pink sheet listings are paid advertisements from market making brokerage firms.

How much time should I spend selecting the penny stocks I'm going to buy?

Many people spend more time shopping for a car than they do buying stocks that could lose their value far more quickly than a car. If you take penny stock investing seriously, and are not just buying the first thing that comes along as a lark, you should spend enough time to research at least several times as many stocks as you intend to buy.

What is the most common problem investors encounter in the penny stock market?

Perhaps the most common complaint among investors in low-priced stocks is that their broker exposed them to an unacceptable level of risk by not fully informing them of how great a chance they stood of losing all their money.

It is obviously wrong for a broker to do this, but investors can easily prevent it from happening to them by carefully researching potential investments rather than trusting entirely in a broker to look out for their interests.

In our experience, many people who lose money (often surprisingly large sums) in penny stocks have never invested in securities before and have done little research on the stocks they bought. Only when the price of their stocks drop do these people realize their mistake.

Should I buy only those over-the-counter stocks that are listed on the National Association of Securities Dealers Automated Quotation System?

In an effort to distance themselves from the corrupt image of the pink sheet market, some brokerage firms will assure their customers that the over-the-counter stocks they trade are all listed on the NASDAQ system. A NASDAQ listing does provide some assurances about a company's financial condition. But it is no panacea against failure, nor does it guarantee that the stock won't be subject to price manipulation. Careful investigation of the stock and the brokerage firm selling it are essential before buying low-priced NASDAQ or pink sheet stocks.

Do penny stocks behave the same way as stocks traded on the exchanges?

Ordinarily, penny stocks are much less actively traded and thus much less easy to buy and sell than stocks traded on exchanges. They are volatile. A single piece of news can make a stock's price double or sink to nothing.

In the penny stock market, individual market makers have a much greater influence over the price of a stock. Indeed, in some cases they arbitrarily set the price of a stock. Regulators are fond of saying that penny stocks are sold, not bought. Through thousands of phone calls each day, penny stock brokerages can manufacture enormous demand that would not naturally arise among investors. Your task is to identify those companies that can stand on their own.

What is the prospectus?

This document is your most valuable tool in deciding whether to invest in a new stock issue. Before a company can offer stock to the public, it must first file a prospectus with the U.S. Securities and Exchange Commission. The prospectus includes a detailed company history, financial information, biographical information about company officers and the risks associated with the business. By law, it must be available to investors before a stock sale takes place.

Is the prospectus a seal of approval from the SEC?

Definitely not. The SEC simply requires that certain information about a company be contained in a prospectus, it does not approve or disapprove of certain securities.

What is the difference between a Form 10-Q, a Form 10-K, and an annual report?

The 10-Q and 10-K are both required SEC filings. Form 10-Q summarizes a company's most recent fiscal quarter, including income statements, balance sheets and cash flow statements. It also includes other financial information and any legal problems. The 10-K contains similar information for the previous fiscal year. The annual report also contains information from the previous fiscal year. But because it is not a required SEC filing, the annual report may contain more, less or different information from the 10-K.

The company I'm interested in is offering units of common stock and warrants. What are warrants, and should I want them?

Warrants are legal claims to buy common stock issued by a corporation at a certain price within a certain period of time. For example, a company might charge you 50 cents for a unit consisting of one share of common stock and one warrant allowing you to purchase another share of stock for 60 cents before the end of the year.

The young, and often cash-strapped, companies that issue penny stock like to attach warrants to their shares because they are then virtually guaranteed another round of financing as long as their stock price rises. Warrants can be valuable for investors too, but only if the stock price goes up.

What is an income statement?

Income statements summarize company revenues and expenses over a period of time, generally a year or three months (a quarter). They tell you whether your company makes money or not. It is important to make sure a young firm's profits come from operations and not through its investment of the money it raised through going public.

What can the balance sheet tell me that the income statement can't?

The balance sheet shows the financial health of a company at a certain point in time. If a company is losing money, the balance sheet can show how long it can sustain such losses before going out of business.

Where can I find industry average ratios?

Average ratios for different industries are published by Dun & Bradstreet, Standard & Poor's, Robert Morris Associates, and the Federal Trade Commission. Many of these references sources are available at large public libraries.

What is the "spread," and why should I care about it?

The spread is the difference between what your brokerage firm is selling a stock for and what it is willing to pay for it. Spreads on low-priced stocks can be wide, and you shouldn't invest until you know what the spread is.

On a given day, your broker may be selling stock in XYZ company for 10 cents and buying it back for 5 cents. Five cents may not seem like a lot, but it means your stock will have to double in price just for you to break even.

GLOSSARY

Agency trade   security trade in which one brokerage firm that is not a market maker in a stock purchases securities from a market maker for its customer. Customer is charged a commission.

Annual report   yearly report companies send out to shareholders. Contains much of the same information as a *10-K*. Not a required SEC filing.

Arbitration   process in which investor complaints against a brokerage firm are settled by outside arbitrators appointed by the NASD, one of the stock exchanges or the American Arbitration Association.

Asked price   price at which a security is offered for sale on an exchange or in the over-the-counter market. Also called the *offering* price.

Balance sheet   financial statement that lists the assets, liabilities and owners' equity of a business at a specific point in time.

Bid or sell price   highest price a buyer is willing to pay for a security. This is the price a broker pays an investor for his or her stock before a markdown or commission.

Blank check   shell company with no operating business that goes public with the intent of investing in another, unspecified, business.

Blind pool   similar to a *blank check,* except that an ordinary blind pool generally specifies what industry it plans to invest in.

Blue sky laws   state securities regulations.

Boiler room   place where brokers use banks of phones, high pressure sales tactics and lists of potential clients to sell risky or fraudulent securities.

Book value   total value of a company's assets minus its liabilities, as carried on the balance sheet.

Brokerage house firm that buys and sells securities for others. Firms buying and selling stock for investors must be registered with the SEC. Also known as a *broker-dealer*.

Common stock ownership shares in a public corporation with the lowest preference as to assets on liquidation. Holders of common stock have the right to vote for the board of directors.

Churning when a broker trades an account excessively to generate commissions.

Cost of goods sold price a company paid for the tangible goods that it sold.

Current ratio current assets over current liabilities. A company with current assets of $1 million and current liabilities of $500,000 would have a current ratio of 2.

Dilution effects on earnings per share and book value per share if all convertible securities were converted or all rights or stock options were exercised.

Dividend payments by a company to its shareholders.

Due diligence procedure by which underwriter or underwriting syndicate obtains information about company whose stock they are offering to the public.

Earnings per share net income, after taxes, divided by the number of shares outstanding.

8-K form a company must file with the SEC within 15 days of a significant event or change in its business.

Flip refers to a broker-dealer "flipping" a customer out of one stock and into another, often to avoid sending the customer cash profits. Also refers to a situation in which one broker-dealer flips a block of stock to another firm for a set price.

Gross profit net sales minus the cost of goods sold.

Indication of interest expression of desire on the part of an investor to buy shares of a new stock issue that has not yet been cleared by the SEC for sale to the public.

Initial public offering company's first offering of its common stock to the public. Subsequent offerings are known as secondary offerings.

Insiders officers and major shareholders of a corporation.

Inventory finished products or the components of finished products.

Inventory turnover ratio cost of goods sold divided by average inventory. Indicates how many times a company turns over its inventory each year.

Liabilities what a company owes.

Long-term or noncurrent liabilities debt that isn't due for at least a year.

Manipulation scheme to artificially influence the price of a stock.

Markdown amount by which the brokerage firm marks down the price it will pay an investor for his stock from the bid price. This applies only in a *principal* transaction.

Markup amount by which the brokerage firm marks up the price the investor has to pay for a stock from the *asked price.* Also applies only in *principal* transaction.

Market maker brokerage firm that has agreed to buy and sell certain securities and keep an inventory in those securities. Market makers sell stock to the public from their own inventory, marking the price up or down.

NASD self-regulating brokerage industry organization that oversees the over-the-counter market.

NASDAQ National Association of Securities Dealers Automated Quotation System. Electronic system that displays the bid and ask prices offered by dealers around the country for certain over-the-counter securities.

Net sales money a company has received or will receive for goods or services already purchased. Called net sales because it is actually gross sales minus returns and discounts.

Over the counter security that is not listed and traded on an organized exchange.

Par value arbitrary face value assigned to common stock in the equity portion of a company's balance sheet. Bears no relation to market value.

Pink sheets list of about 16,000 over-the-counter securities published daily by the National Quotation Bureau Inc. In the pink sheets, market makers list their bid and ask prices for the securities they trade.

Preferred stock security that pays a fixed return, and whose owners must be paid before common stock holders.

Preliminary prospectus initial prospectus for the sale of securities. Red print advises customers that this is not the final prospectus.

Present value value today of some payment to be received in the future.

Price to earnings ratio market price of a company's common stock divided by its earnings per common share.

Principal trade brokerage firm buys stock directly from you for its inventory or sells it to you directly out of its own inventory.

Prospectus official document describing a new securities issue. It must be furnished to investors.

Quarterly report financial report companies are required to file with the SEC four times each year; also known as the 10-Q.

Red herring see *preliminary prospectus*.

Reverse split opposite of a stock split. The number of shares is reduced rather than increased. For example, a company might give investors one share for the 10 they now own. Reverse splits are common in the penny stock market, where companies often have an enormous number of outstanding shares.

Right privilege granted to existing shareholders by a company wishing to sell more stock. Gives existing shareholders the right to buy stock in the new offering before it is offered to the public.

172

Risk   volatility of an investment.

Risk tolerance   degree to which an investor can accept different levels of risk.

Secondary offering   offerings of stock to the public subsequent to the *initial offering.*

Script   sales pitch written out for a broker.

Shell   public company with no operating business.

Spread   difference between the *bid price* and the *asked price* on a stock.

Stock manipulation   artificial scheme designed to affect the price and trading volume of certain securities.

Stock split   division of already outstanding shares. For example, a two-for-one split would double the amount of stock each shareholder owned.

Street name   when an investor does not take delivery of his stock certificates, but leaves them with his brokerage firm, the stock is said to be registered in street name.

13-D   SEC document that tells who owns more than 5 percent of a company's stock. If an individual or institution is accumulating a great deal of stock, it may signal a takeover attempt.

U.S. Securities and Exchange Commission (SEC) federal agency created to administer the Securities Acts of 1933 and 1934. Oversees the securities industry.

Underwriter   firm that has agreed to sell a new stock issue to the public.

Underwriting syndicate   group of firms selling new stock issue.

Units   increments in which common stock and warrants are sold in a public offering. For example, a company might be selling 1 million units each consisting of four shares of stock and one *warrant.*

Warrant   allows investor to buy a certain amount of a stock at a certain price by a certain date. Often sold in units with *common stock* in penny stock offerings.

INDEX

174